URBAN LEGENDS

The Truth Behind All Those
Deliciously Entertaining Myths
That Are Absolutely, Positively,
100% Not True!

By Richard Roeper

CAREER
PRESS

FRANKLIN
LAKES, NJ

URBAN LEGENDS
Cover design by Cheryl Finbow
Printed in the U.S.A. by Book-mart Press

To order this title, please call toll-free 1-800-CAREER-1 (NJ and Canada: 201-848-0310) to order using VISA or Mastercard, or for further information on books from Career Press.

The Career Press, Inc., 3 Tice Road, PO Box 687, Franklin Lakes, NJ 07417

Library of Congress Cataloging-in-Publication Data

Roeper, Richard.

   Urban legends : the truth behind all those deliciously entertaining myths that are absolutely, positively, 100 percent not true / by Richard Roeper.
   p.   cm.
   ISBN 1-56414-418-6 (hc.)

   1. Urban folklore—United States.   2. United States—Social life and customs.   I. Title.
GR105.R64   1999
398.2'0973'091732—dc21

                                                  99-30958
                                                  CIP

Acknowledgments

It took me six months to write this book. It also took me 25 years. I've been hearing and telling urban legends for at least a quarter of a century—and I've been lucky enough to know hundreds of people who share my enthusiasm for these wonderful, if completely bogus, stories. Though space considerations prevent me from naming everyone, I would like to thank the following people for their friendship, guidance, support and encouragement as I worked on this book:

My agent, Sheree Bykofsky, and her terrific associate, Janet Rosen; at Career Press, my editor, Darren Bergstein, who sculpted the project into its existing shape, and Anne Brooks; Nigel Wade, Larry Green, Joyce Winnecke, the library staff and the many editors at the *Chicago Sun-Times*, who have understood and tolerated my near-obsession with the urban legend as column subject over the years. Special thanks to Steve Huntley, who was my editor on many, many urban legend-related columns.

Much appreciation and gratitude goes to Michelle Carney, who provided an invaluable contribution as a researcher and fact-checker on this book.

Thanks to Lynn and Nick Zona; Bob and Colleen Roeper; Laura Roeper; Laura LeQuesne; John LeQuesne; Sam Saunders; Emily Roeper; Caroline Roeper; Carla Lang; Paige Smoron; Bill Adee; Neil Steinberg; Phil Rosenthal; Bill Zwecker; Robert Feder; Sherri Gilman; Anita Huslin; Susan Axelrod; Dennis Britton; Carolee Morrison; Bebe Lerner; Julia Wallace; Jennifer Weigel; Ken Swanborn; Michael Cavoto; Pam Johnson; Rick Kogan; Jim Wiser; Jacqueline Colbert; Drew Hayes; Leslie Baldacci; and Stephanie Dee.

Heartfelt appreciation goes to the many colleagues and to the hundreds of readers who have passed along tips about urban legends old and new.

This book is dedicated to my parents, Robert and Margaret Roeper, who believed in the art of storytelling at the dinner table, and whose marriage of more than 40 years proves that love is not an urban myth.

Contents

Introduction

Be honest now. What was your reaction the first time you heard the remarks made by Tommy Hilfiger on *The Oprah Winfrey Show*? You were stunned and outraged, no doubt. How could such a well-respected designer utter such ignorant, racist comments, on Oprah's show of all places? He deserved to get tossed off the set!

You also believed every word of the story, didn't you? Didn't see the show yourself, but you figured it must have happened. That's why you couldn't resist telling your friends.

The problem is, it never happened. When you passed along the gossip about Hilfiger, you were unwittingly feeding the many-headed, insatiable beast known as the modern urban legend. Each retelling of a tale gives the monster another ounce of energy.

No need to apologize. We're all hopeless gossips at heart. The moment we hear a story that's too good to be true (and that's usually because it is too good to be true), we log onto our computers, dash for the fax machines, and lunge for the telephone to share the item with a few trusted friends—who then duplicate the sequence with a few more acquaintances, and so on, and so on. Within a matter of hours, a devilishly hatched, anonymously circulated untruth can ricochet around the globe and be absorbed by millions of people, quickly taking root as firm fact and living for years despite all noble efforts to set the record straight.

Modern technology has only served to speed up this process. One school of thought suggested that the Internet, with its power to inform the masses, would help to weed out bogus tales and debunk long-standing myths. What has happened is quite the opposite. The technology that enables a college student in New Zealand to communicate with a high school sophomore in Nebraska, who then passes on the story to a cyberspace pen pal in Tokyo, has put the modern urban legend on fast-forward, zipping around the planet at a breakneck pace.

Additionally, the Internet has proved to be a fertile landscape for the endless circulation of phony press releases, doctored documents, concocted quotations and "news stories" falsely attributed to legitimate organizations and/or nonexistent newspapers and wire services. Where it used to take weeks, months, even years for an urban legend to travel around the world (via party conversation, water cooler gossip, and chain letters), it can be a matter of hours before everyone from New York to Honolulu to London to Beijing is familiar with the shocking story of the young man who picked up the attractive woman in a bar and took her back to his hotel room for unprotected sex, only to wake up the next morning to see a chilling message on his bathroom mirror: WELCOME TO THE WONDERFUL WORLD OF AIDS. (Thought that one was true, too, didn't you? Not so.)

As we enter the millennium, we're supposedly smarter, better informed and less willing to believe everything we read. But if that's the case, why do millions of people pass on e-mail chain letters and repeat celebrity urban legends without stopping for one moment to consider if there's any truth to what they've heard? Today's information consumer is savvy, jaded, and cynical, yet as willing as ever to believe stories that happened to "my best friend's brother's accountant."

The same audience that creates web sites devoted to urban legends, the same hipsters who chuckle knowingly at the irony-laced references to modern folklore in movies such as *Scream, Scream 2, Dead Man on Campus, Dead Man's Curve,* and of course, *Urban Legend,* excitedly, passionately, stubbornly insist that Keanu Reeves really did get married on the beach in Malibu to media mogul David Geffen, that rocker Marilyn Manson really did play Kevin's best friend on *The Wonder Years,* and that Bill Gates really is offering $1,000 to the first 1,000 people who respond to his e-mail message, and we've got to do something about it, dammit!

After you read this book, you'll have intimate knowledge of many of the most popular urban legends in circulation—but you must use this knowledge carefully. Nobody likes a showoff.

For more than a decade, I've been tracking urban legends on a regular basis in my *Chicago Sun-Times* column, which is syndicated by the *New York Times* syndicate to a number of newspapers across the country. Nearly every month, I hear about a new urban legend, or I'm alerted to the resurgence of a classic. Sometimes the reader who contacts me is hip to the game and is alerting me to the latest tall tale making the rounds; but more often I receive misguided "urgent messages" or "hot tips" from readers exhorting me to rush into print the shocking news that AIDS-infected drug addicts are leaving tainted needles in the coin slots of pay phones, or gangs are flashing their headlights at unsuspecting drivers in a deadly initiation rite.

I try to fight the good fight. Every few months or so, I pinpoint the particularly popular urban legends making the rounds and I do my best to debunk them via common sense, factual evidence, denials from relevant parties, etc. It's always satisfying to hear from grateful readers who have circulated the column on the Internet or tacked it to the company bulletin board with a note attached that reads, I TOLD YOU GUYS THIS WASN'T TRUE. I like to think I've saved a few people from swallowing and repeating the latest piece of irresistible fiction disguised as fact.

Then again, I can't tell you how many times I've written about an urban legend only to hear from literally hundreds of people who seem to think I've confirmed the story and would like a copy to show to their friends. Sigh.

I've come to believe there are two kinds of people in this world: Those who embrace far too many urban legends (or ULs) as fact and delight in sharing them with everyone in their lives, and those who immediately recognize ULs on sight and would dearly like to read an authoritative, modern work that will assist them in their debunking efforts. A nicely packaged hardcover book, like the one you're holding, for example.

This book is for both groups. The aim here is not to mock or belittle anyone for believing even the most preposterous story; heck, I've fallen for a number of them myself over the years, including the disgusting UL about the honeymooners who are victimized by burglars who perform a nasty stunt with the couple's toothbrushes and record it on film. (I still swear that happened to my ex-girlfriend's co-worker's friends…well, maybe not.)

While it's essentially impossible to completely disprove a UL with 100 percent certainty that it hasn't occurred, I'll come as close as possible to explaining why some of your favorite urban legends just couldn't have taken place anywhere in the real world. Not that we don't wish that all these stories were true. Think of how much more fun it would be if they were based in reality! It would be fascinating (in an *X-Files* kind of way) to live in a world in which James Dean gave a Harley to Elvis and Neil Armstrong issued a secret message to his old neighbor when he set foot on the moon, where a ghost is captured on video in *Three Men and A Baby*, and where brides dramatically exit rehearsal dinners after announcing the groom slept with the maid of honor...

But the truth should count for something, shouldn't it?

Chapter One
The Classics

No, you won't find the story of the ghostly hitchhiker or the killer with a hook-hand here; those golden oldies have been told and retold in dozens of books about folklore and in hundreds of ancient newspaper and magazine stories. Some of the urban legends included in this chapter do have roots extending back 20 years or more, but many of them were created and gained widespread popularity only in the last few years, and nearly all of them are still believed to be true by many people...

"They're stealing our kidneys!"

A married business traveler fancied himself quite the studmuffin, and every time he went on a trip, he'd seek the company of sexually adventurous young women. After attending a convention in New Orleans, he hit Bourbon Street after a long day of meetings and seminars. Hopping from bar to bar, slugging down potent drinks such as Hurricanes and Hand Grenades, the guy got hammered and amorous, and was determined to stay on the prowl until he found some companionship.

His persistence paid off. Deep into the night, he hooked up with a gorgeous, exotic woman who downed some tequila with him, rubbed her hands all over him, licked his ear and finally suggested they retreat to his hotel room. The guy figured he was scoring for sure, and he eagerly took her up on the offer. They raced out of the bar and dashed for his hotel, where they proceeded to make out in the elevator like a couple of teenagers on prom night. They stumbled down the hallway and made their way to the guy's room. Once inside, she offered to make him one last drink before they ripped their clothes off.

That's the last thing he remembered. The next morning, he woke up in the bathtub, submerged in ice, freezing to death. A telephone had been placed on a small table next to the tub, and there was a note taped to the wall telling him to call 911 when he awoke. Still dazed, his head pounding and his body aching, the guy managed to pick up the phone. He started to explain what happened, but apparently the operator had heard this story before, because she cut him off and instructed him to slowly, carefully reach behind him to feel if there was a tube protruding from his lower back. To his horror, the man discovered just such a tube. But what did it mean?

"Stay still," the 911 operator told him in a calm, forceful voice. "Paramedics are already on their way. One of your kidneys has been stolen."

🔹 🔹 🔹

If all the kidneys that supposedly have been harvested by black market thieves really *were* swiped, there would be a mountain of kidneys piled high in some mysterious warehouse somewhere, and hospitals from New Orleans to New York would be filled with kidney-less victims—but of course that's not the case.

Though these kidney-stealing stories have been circulating for years, I've been unable to uncover one legitimate news account of such an incident, nor are there any medical journals, police reports or hospital records confirming that the story has any grounds in reality. Nevertheless, the kidney-harvesting tale sprouts up like a poisonous mushroom every couple of years, almost invariably in a city that is either a popular tourist stop such as Las Vegas or a convention city such as Atlanta or Chicago.

And Hollywood loves this story. Kidney-swiping storylines have appeared on at least two network series: *The X-Files* and *Law and Order*. There's also a weirdly entertaining little 1993 thriller called *Harvest* that used the story as a launching point.

Over the last three years, fliers, faxes, and Internet warnings about gangs of kidney-stealers have periodically popped up all over New Orleans, usually just before the start of the Mardi Gras festivities. Lieutenant Martin Defillo of the New Orleans Police Department told me he's been fielding calls for more than three years." And still there is no credible information to support [stories of] kidney stealing," he said. "I adamantly believe this is a hoax."

The N.O.P.D. even issued an official notice in an effort to ease the fears of locals and tourists alike. It reads (in part): "The past few months the New Orleans Police Department has received numerous inquiries from corporations and organizations around the United States warning travelers about a well-organized crime ring operating in New Orleans. This information alleges that this ring steals kidneys from travelers after they have been provided alcohol to the point of unconsciousness. After an investigation into these matters, the New Orleans Police Department has found them to be *completely without merit and without foundation*. The warnings...are *fictitious* and may be in violation of criminal statutes concerning the issuance of erroneous and misleading information."

Sometimes, the kidney-stealing urban legend is cloaked in a morality tale, i.e., "This happened to a married guy who let this woman into his hotel room," but just as often the victim is an innocent tourist whose only mistake is letting someone buy him a drink in a bar in a strange town.

It's also a neat little chiller of a horror story—the notion that scalpel-wielding amateur surgeons will cut vital organs right out of your body and sell them to desperate patients willing to fork over thousands of dollars—but it's also completely absurd once you follow the story to its inevitable conclusion. If there are hundreds of people stealing kidneys, doesn't that mean there would have to be a number of medical facilities that would accept these ill-gotten organs, and dozens of doctors willing to perform the transplants.

According to experts, the process of removing a kidney, transporting it, and successfully placing it in another host is so incredibly complicated that it would be virtually impossible unless a team of highly trained medical experts performed the feat.

Tina Weiss, patient services coordinator for the National Kidney Foundation, said, "There is no way this could happen, because the organ donation process is very complex." Weiss explained that in order for a kidney to take, you first have to have a certain kind of match, which is why blood relatives are usually the best possible donors. If a stranger provides a kidney, chances are it won't take—not to mention the immediate escalation of white blood cell counts when foreign tissue is introduced to an immune system, the high risk of infection, and the incredible loss of blood that would occur if someone were to slice into someone's lower back.

In reality, our hypothetical stud wouldn't wake up to find a message telling him to call 911—he'd be dead.

Dr. Wendy Brown, chairman of the National Kidney Foundation, said of the kidney story, "It's an urban myth run amok. In truth, transplanting a kidney from a living donor involves numerous tests for compatibility that must be performed before the kidney is removed. It's highly unlikely that a gang could operate in secrecy to recover organs that would be viable for a transplant." According to the United Network for Organ Sharing, "There is absolutely no evidence of such activity ever occurring in the U.S. or any other industrialized country. While the tale sounds credible enough for many listeners, it has no basis in the reality of organ transplantation."

So what are the odds that some chick in a slinky gown will slip you a mickey, take you back to your hotel room, neatly slice out your kidney and leave you in a tub of ice? Let's just say you have a better chance of flapping your arms and flying.

UL FOOTNOTE. In 1994, a variation of this story reached Guatemala, where the locals believed rumors that Americans and Europeans were coming to their country to kidnap their children to steal their kidneys. As a result, a number of tourists were actually attacked and beaten by Guatemalans. On March 29, 1994, an American tourist was rushed by a mob who accused her of abducting a Guatemalan boy for the purpose of stealing his internal organs. She was beaten severely, suffering broken arms, internal injuries and severe head trauma, and was in a coma for more than a month.

Dog swallows cell phone

On Christmas morning, as Lucky, her beloved labrador retriever, frolics in the background and her favorite carols play on the stereo, a young woman opens a present from her husband: a brand new cellular phone, the smallest and most technologically advanced model on the market. As her excited spouse demonstrates all of the phone's features, she feigns great interest while thinking, "What, no jewelry?" (He even charged the phone and programmed it for her so she could use it right away.)

"That's great," says the young woman, as she continues unwrapping her gifts.

After all the presents have been opened, she collects the wrapping paper and ribbons for the garbage, and that's when she realizes the phone is missing. She sees the box, the charger, and the owners' manual, but the phone itself can't be found. "That phone is too small, I've lost it already," she says to her husband.

"Don't worry, we'll find it," he replies, but even after they dump the trash on the ground and sift through it, there's no phone.

"Wait!" cries the husband. "I already programmed *your* new number into *my* cell phone, and I turned on the ringer on your phone, so I'll just dial you up and we'll hear the phone ring and locate it that way."

"You're a genius," says the wife.

The husband takes out his phone and punches up his wife's number, and sure enough, they hear the phone ringing.

"It's coming from somewhere near Lucky," she says as her dog looks at her with the saddest expression in the world. "He must have buried it in the nativity scene. Look how guilty he looks."

The phone keeps ringing, as her husband digs around under the tree.

"I can't find it," he says.

"I don't understand," says his wife. "I can hear it. It's coming from right under Lucky."

And then it dawns on her husband. He holds his ear to the dog's belly, and his worst fears are confirmed. "Honey," he says. "The phone isn't near Lucky. It's *in* Lucky. He swallowed it."

Needless to say, the poor dog has quite the tummy ache. The wife calls the veterinarian, but in her panic she leaves her new cell phone number instead of their home number, and when the vet calls back, Lucky's stomach rings again.

"Would somebody please answer the dog!" says her husband, trying to make light of things. His wife is not amused.

Eventually they're able to reach the vet, who tells them there's really nothing that can be done other than "allowing Mother Nature to take its course." Later that day, Lucky goes into the backyard and deposits the usual droppings, along with the new phone. Amazingly, it still works!

The *Sun*, a London tabloid, ran just such a story in late 1997: "Rachel Murray, 27, had left the cell phone under her Christmas tree as a surprise gift for her roommate. But her friend Tony Dangerfield's bloodhound, Charlie, crept into the room and greedily wolfed down the mobile phone, leaving only a pile of torn paper. After a frantic search for the phone, Murray obtained the number from the telephone company, dialed it and heard muffled ringing from sleeping Charlie's stomach. The dog was rushed to a vet, who advised Murray and Dangerfield to let nature take its course. Twenty-four hours later the phone dutifully emerged—in perfect working order."

The tabloid even ran a picture of the gal, the dog, and the phone, which was a fairly large-sized model, about the same size as the woman's hand.

⊠ ⊠ ⊠

Could a dog swallow a cellular phone?

Well, he'd have to be an awfully big dog and it would have to be an awfully small phone. Maybe if some ferocious beast were able to chew the plastic device down to smaller pieces it could happen, but in that scenario, the phone certainly wouldn't still be working. Even if the world's largest St. Bernard managed to swallow a cell phone whole, how would the phone work its way through the dog's intestinal tract? And even if the world's largest St. Bernard swallowed the world's smallest cellular phone and it somehow worked its way through the dog's digestive system and was deposited in a big pile in the backyard, who in the world is going to fetch that phone, clean it off and test it to see if it still works?

My attempts to locate the so-called Ms. Murray and Mr. Dangerfield were unsuccessful. Had I been able to locate Ms. Murray, I would have asked her:

1. If the cellular phone was a gift, how did you manage to charge it so that it would ring? Did you take it out of the box, charge it and then put everything back?

2. Why was the phone turned on?

3. Why did you have to obtain the number from the phone company? If you had signed up your friend to a phone service, wouldn't you have the number?

4. And...did you really want to keep the phone, after all it had been through?

The truth about Furbys

Furby it from me to pass along unsubstantiated rumors about the most popular toy of the 1998 holiday season; my mission is not to spread untruths, but to clear up bogus information.

Several Furby-related stories have been making the rounds. (Say what you will about the Furby, but what urban legends were inspired by Tickle Me Elmo or the Cabbage Patch Kids?) Most of these tales are concocted from pure silliness, but one has a basis in truth, even though that truth springs from a myth.

In December of 1998, the National Security Agency issued an internal memo banning Furbys from its Fort Meade, Maryland headquarters for reasons of, well, national security. As the *Washington Post* reported, "The supersecret spy agency put out a 'Furby Alert' on its internal message system in early December and banned Furbys."

The memo reportedly stated, in part: "Personally owned photographic, video and audio recording equipment are prohibited items. This includes toys, such as 'Furbys,' with built-in recorders that repeat the audio with synthesized sound to mimic the original."

In the *Post*'s story, a "Capitol Hill source" said the NSA was worried "that people would take them home and they'd start talking classified."

Sounds crazy, doesn't it? Actually, that part of the story is absolutely true. The NSA did issue that memo, and employees really are prohibited from bringing their Furby friends to work, but the spy agency's information on Furbys is incorrect, as the $30 toys do *not* have the capability of recording anything.

"[The NSA memo] gave us the biggest chuckle," said Lana Simon, director of public relations for Tiger Electronics, the Vernon Hills, Illinois company that manufactures Furbys. "We were amazed that the government apparently didn't test a Furby to see if it records conversations," said Simon. "Nor did anyone from the NSA call us. If they had, we would have explained that Furbys do not have recording devices installed in them. The toys are preprogrammed to speak in English and in a language called 'Furbish.' The way in which you play with the Furby will determine how the Furby will react, but the Furby will not mimic anything you say to it."

Tiger Electronics President Roger Shiffman issued a statement: "Although Furby is a clever toy, it does not record or mimic voices...The NSA did not do their homework. Furby is not a spy! You can talk to it until your face turns blue and it will never store a word or kick it back to you at a later date."

The NSA wasn't the only organization that didn't grasp this fundamental fact about the Furby. The *Washington Post* and other news agencies were quick to pounce on the NSA memo as a fun story about government bureaucracy, but as far as I could determine, nobody indicated that the memo wasn't needed because a Furby isn't a tape recorder.

"No, the *Post* didn't call us either," said Simon. "They just ran with [the story]."

In March of 1999, Simon called me with an update. "The saga continues," she said. "Now it's the Navy banning Furbys!" Sure enough, the United States Navy had banned Furbys from restricted areas at the Norfolk, Virginia Naval Shipyard and other Navy bases, claiming that "Furby is a recording device...and a security violation." Tiger Electronics President Shiffman responded, "Since Furby is so lifelike, it tends to inspire imaginations. Again, Furby is not a spy."

This is not to say that only government security agencies and newspapers believe Furbys have recording capabilities and/or a "memory" of sorts. Many wild claims have been made about the learning capacity of Furbys, from the woman who swears her Furby speaks Italian to her, to the Furby-files who say their toys can sing opera. (Then there are the phony tales circulating about "rare" Furbys with peculiar markings or black-and-white fur.)(It all falls under the category of wishful thinking.)

And what scares you more: that the National Security Agency couldn't decipher how a Furby works, or that NSA employees were so attached to the toys that a memo banning them had to be issued in the first place?

ⓧ ⓧ ⓧ

Of course, the *true* Furby scandal has to do with their fur, which is made from real cat and dog fur.

That's right: DNA tests have confirmed this horrible secret. The Humane Society has issued a press release condemning the manufacturer for engaging in such a disgusting and unspeakably cruel technique just to make Furbys seem more "real."

This UL is 100 percent false. There's no half-truth or spark of truth, or any hint of the truth here.

"The DNA issue, that one really threw us for a loop," said Simon. "Apparently someone altered a Humane Society press release, but as soon as the real organization found out about it, they issued a statement saying the information was untrue and they were not behind it."

From the Humane Society: "A press release...under the Humane Society of the United States name stated an HSUS investigation found that Furby toys were made with dog and cat fur. We did not issue this press release and want to state very clearly that this information is untrue..."

So Furby fur is made from...what?

"It's 100 percent acrylic," said Simon. "A lot of acrylics were killed in the name of Furbys."

I think the National Security Agency should look into this.

Prehistoric Barbie

Seems there was this drugged-out old hippie in California who used to be an archaeology professor before drugs fried his mind, reducing him to a babbling eccentric who putters around his house and keeps the TV on at all hours. The guy had this habit of digging in the abandoned lot behind his house, unearthing all sorts of garbage and then sending his "prehistoric findings" to the Smithsonian Institution: old soda bottles, pieces of rusted pipe, you name it.

Once, the guy dug up the head of a Barbie doll, and in his altered state he sent it to the Smithsonian with a long note explaining his theories about his rare find. Some low-level bureaucrat at the Smithsonian, obviously fed up with this clown, sent him the following letter:

Dear Sir:

Thank you for your latest submission labeled "211-D, Layer Seven, next to the clothesline post, Hominid Skull." We have given this specimen a careful examination, and regret to inform you that we disagree with your theory that it represents "conclusive proof of the existence of early man in Los Angeles two million years ago."

Rather, it appears that what you found is the head of a Barbie doll, of the variety one of our staff believes to be "Malibu Barbie." It is evident you have given a great deal of thought to the analysis of this specimen, and you may be quite certain that those of us who are familiar with your prior work in the field were loathe to contradict your findings. However, we do feel there are a number of physical attributes which might have tipped you off to its modern origin:

1. The material is molded plastic. Ancient hominid remains are typically fossilized bone.

2. The cranial capacity of the specimen is approximately 9 cubic centimeters, well below the threshold of even the earliest identified proto-hominids.

3. The dentition pattern evident on the "skull" is more consistent with the common domesticated dog than it is with the "ravenous man-eating Pliocene clams" you speculate roamed the wetlands during that time.

It is with feelings tinged with melancholy that we must deny your request to have the specimen carbon-dated. This is partially due to the heavy load our lab must bear in its normal operation, and partly due to carbon dating's notorious inaccuracy in fossils of recent geological record. To the best of our knowledge, no Barbie dolls were produced prior to 1956 A.D., and carbon dating is likely to produce wildly inaccurate results.

However, we gladly accept your generous donation of this specimen to our museum. While it is undoubtedly not a hominid fossil, it is, nonetheless, yet another riveting example of the great body of work you have accumulated here so effortlessly.

You should know that our director has reserved a special shelf in his own office for the display of the specimens you have previously submitted to the Institution, and the entire staff speculates daily on what you will happen upon next in your dig.

We eagerly anticipate your trip to the nation's capital that you proposed in your latest letter, and several of us are pressing the director to pay for it. We are particularly interested in hearing you expand on theories surrounding the "trans-positating fillifitation of ferrous ions in a structural matrix" that makes the excellent juvenile T-Rex femur you recently sent us take on the deceptive appearance of a rusty 9mm. Sears Craftsman automotive crescent wrench.

Yours in Science,
Harvey Rowe, Curator, Antiquities
Smithsonian Institute
1500 W. Pennsylvania, Washington, D.C.

Randall Kramer is the public affairs director for the Smithsonian. "I've been hearing that story for more than five years now," he said. "It's a clumsily written but clever letter circulating on the Internet. For the record, there never has been a Harvey Rowe at the Smithsonian—and by the way it's the Smithsonian Institution, not Smithsonian Institute— and it's not located on Pennsylvania Avenue."

I'll make a note of that. Want to make sure I have the correct address when I send them the G.I. Joe I found in my backyard.

Gang initiation rites

A woman who lived in a posh suburb of Chicago was driving into the city when she saw a car approaching in the outbound lane with its lights off. Concerned about the driver's safety, the woman politely flashed her brights at the oncoming car to let him know his lights weren't on. The driver blinked his lights in gratitude as it passed by, and the woman felt good about doing a small favor for a fellow motorist. She pretty much forgot about the episode until about 10 minutes later, when, on a rather quiet side street, she noticed a car riding her bumper—a car that looked an awful lot like the vehicle she had signaled earlier!

Strangely, the car's lights were once again off. This wasn't right. In the woman's rearview mirror, she could make out the silhouettes of the driver and numerous passengers, all of whom were young black men wearing hats and baseball jackets. Their car stereo was booming so loud she could practically feel it, even though her windows were rolled up. They seemed to be passing around a bottle.

The woman could feel her heart pounding. What had she done wrong? What did they want with her?

A moment later, she found out. The car pulled alongside her, and the driver motioned for the woman to roll down her window. Smiling bravely, she cooperated, hoping that the young men wished her no harm; maybe they wanted to tell her she had a busted taillight or a tire that was going flat. But those hopes vanished in a horrific instant, as the rear driver's side window rolled down and one of them pointed a shotgun at the woman, squeezing the trigger before she even had a chance to scream. As the dead woman's car careened into a nearby light pole, the young man in the back seat exchanged high-five's and accepted congratulations from the other punks in the car.

"Your initiation is over," said the driver. "You're now in the gang."

The poor woman, a churchgoing mother of three, had become the latest innocent victim of a gang initiation rite that has been enacted in major urban areas across the country. So whatever you do when you're driving, if you see someone whose lights are off—*ignore it*. Flashing your brights in an effort to play Good Samaritan could get you killed.

The flashing-headlight story has traversed the country like a Smashing Pumpkins tour, landing everywhere from New York to Los Angeles.

When the rumors surfaced in Chicago a few years ago, I contacted a detective in the Gang Crimes Unit of the Chicago Police Deptartment, who laughed and said not only had it never happened, but nearly every element of the story goes against everything police know about the way gangs operate.

"Gang leaders are a lot of things, but they aren't stupid," the detective told me. "The one thing they don't want to do is draw attention to themselves. If they were picking off innocent motorists on highways and streets that are way outside their turf, how long do you think it would be before they'd be put away? Everyone from the mayor to the chief of police on down would make nabbing them a number one priority. And let's not even talk about all the media coverage something like that would generate."

An exhaustive search of newspaper articles nationwide turned up not one single report of any such crime occurring (although stories about rumors of such activity have been around since 1993). That's because as far as anyone has been able to determine, there's never been a gang initiation involving flashing headlights. "They have gang initiations, all right," said the Chicago detective. "What usually happens is that everybody beats the crap out of the new guy. That's the extent of the typical gang initiation."

The big fear over the years has been that some gang will enact the flashing-headlight scenario precisely *because* they've heard the urban legend. As far as I can tell, that hasn't happened yet, but I do know an awful lot of people who refuse to flash their lights at other drivers even as they acknowledge that the story probably isn't true.

Perhaps even more widely known is the gang-initiation ritual involving "pledges" who hide under vehicles at malls and slash the ankles of unsuspecting shoppers. It's only a matter of time before this story appears in a horror movie, as the visuals are too sickeningly perfect:

A stylish and attractive young woman drives her BMW to an upscale mall in the suburbs after work. By the time she emerges from the mall, darkness has set in, and she feels just a slight chill of fear as she high-heels it back to her car. She takes out her key chain with the remote alarm; the doors unlock and the headlights flash and the car beeps as she looks around to make sure no one is following her.

All is clear. She puts the bags in the back seat, slams the door shut, opens the driver's door and has one foot already in the vehicle. Suddenly she feels a hand clamped vise-like around her left leg, and a sharp, fiery sensation as the attacker slashes her ankle, causing her to collapse in pain so great she can't even call out for help. The assailant—a wiry teenager—scrambles out from under the car, takes the woman's packages and scampers into the night, the blood gleaming from his switchblade as proof that he has completed the last rite of initiation into his neighborhood gang.

Bulletin board rumors, Internet warnings, faxed "reports" and word-of-mouth gossip about supposed ankle-slashings have appeared in dozens of cities large and small, but once again, there's no factual evidence to confirm that this has ever happened, even once. (Not that this stopped advice columnist Abigail Van Buren—Dear Abby—from printing an ankle-slashing rumor in 1992, along with a warning to her readers to be extra-careful when visiting their local malls.)

Although it's not usually stated explicitly, there's a form of racism at work here. The victims in these two urban legends are almost invariably described as "suburban women" (i.e., whites) while the attackers are "inner-city gangbangers," (i.e., young black males). Like many urban legends, these stories prey on the fear some whites have of black gangs. That's the none-too-subtle message behind the "gang initiation" urban legends.

Tainted needles

A woman is driving through a dangerous neighbor hood when her cell phone battery conks out right in the middle of an important business call. Her instincts tell her to keep driving until she reaches her office, but she doesn't want her client to think she hung up on him, so she reluctantly pulls into a parking lot containing a phone booth. Once inside, she places her call without incident—until she reflexively puts her index finger in the coin slot to see if there's any spare change, and feels a sharp jabbing pain. She withdraws her finger and sees that it's bleeding—and when she peers into the coin slot she discovers to her horror that someone has left aused hypodermic needle in there!

The poor woman rushes to her doctor, who performs a series of blood tests. A while later, she receives the tragic news: She's HIV-positive.

⊠ ⊠ ⊠

The needles-in-the-coin-slot story seems to be a new one. I couldn't find any reference to it before the fall of 1998, but in a very short time it has become one of the most frequently repeated stories on the Internet and gossip circuit. However, it could very well be inspired by an old urban legend in which a woman goes shopping at her local department store and feels a "pin prick" while rummaging through a pile of sweaters. The pin prick turns out to be a fatal bite from a viper who arrived with a shipment of goods from Asia. More recently, there have been tales of kids at rave parties or moviegoers who have been stuck by AIDS-tainted needles.

Here's a typical Internet posting of the needles-in-the-coin-slot rumor, dated Nov. 14, 1998:

"This [message] was sent to me by a very good friend who works for CDC (Center for Disease Control):

SUBJECT: FYI - Don't Use That Telephone!

This is serious! VERY IMPORTANT INFORMATION! ALERT! ALERT!

"There is something new happening that everyone should be aware of. Drug users are now taking their used needles and putting them into the coin return slots of public telephones. People are putting their fingers in to recover coins or just to check to see if anyone left loose change and are getting stuck by needles infected with hepatitis, HIV and other diseases. This message is posted to make everyone aware of the danger. The change isn't worth it!

"P.S. This information came straight from phone company workers...this did NOT come from hearsay or an urban legend source."

Of course, the sender somehow forgot to include some pertinent details, like the date and location of any such incidents, the names of any victims or phone company sources for the story...little things like that.

Here's another Internet posting:

"A friend of a friend is currently going through EMT (Emergency Medical Technician) class and they've been warned to be very careful reaching in any slot for return change. I guess the latest 'thing' is placing hypodermic needles into change-return slots, causing people to get pricked when they reach in for their change. These needles are showing up primarily at public pay phones, but obviously it could spread easily and quickly [to] stamp machines, vending machines, etc. "Please be careful. Thanks for your attention."

This hoary tale falls under the broad umbrella of AIDS-fear urban legends. Even if you're living a clean life, so the story goes, you're at risk of contracting this horrible disease simply by using a pay phone and checking for spare change! Is it possible something like this could have happened? Maybe—it's not beyond the realm of possibility to imagine some pathetic idiot or goofball prankster leaving a used needle in a coin slot. It's more likely that the offender would be *inspired* by the story already making the rounds. In fact, that seems to be what happened in 1999 in Wythe County, Virginia, when hypodermic needles were found in post office mail slots, a night deposit box, and a pay telephone slot. The victims in each incident were taken to hospitals and treated, but no one suffered serious injuries or infections.

Wythe County Chief Deputy Sam Viars said that the rash of incidents happened only after the circulation of a pamphlet warning about (at the time, non-existent) episodes of tainted needles being planted in pay phone slots. It appears somebody got the idea after reading about what had been only a myth.

Urban Legends

In an article in the *Roanoke Times*, Herb Cooley, the police chief of Pulaski, Virginia, said police hadn't determined if the needles found in coin slots in his town had been placed there by a jokester, but he said, "No one is laughing...You hear this stuff about urban legends and people say, 'That never happens here.' Well, now it has happened here."

Copycats aside, 99.9 percent of the stories about tainted needles in coin slots are pure fiction.

The Gerber rebate

In the fall of 1997, I received the following fax at my office at the *Sun-Times*, reproduced here with grammatical tics and awkward phrasing intact.

Reported 8/20/97 (Reuters News Service)

Gerber Baby Food has lost a class action law suit against them. Gerber has been marketing Gerber has been marketing their baby food as "all natural" but in fact they had used preservatives. In the settlement they are responsible for giving every child (under the age of 12) born between 1985 and 1997 a $500 Savings Bond. As part of the settlement Gerber is not responsible for contacting or advertising the settlement in any way whatsoever. If you have or know anyone who has a child born during the timeframe, this will be valuable information to them. Please pass it along. To obtain the bond, send a copy of the child's birth certificate and social security card direct to:

Gerber Food

Settlement Administration, Infant Litigation

P. O. Box 1602, Minneapolis, MN 56180

In another version of the letter, people were advised to send both their e-mail addresses and $2 in order to receive their rebates.

Hundreds of thousands of parents received these faxes and dutifully sent their claims to the post office box number on the fax. Then they waited for their $500 savings bonds.

They're still waiting.

Like many urban legends, this one sprouted from a murky mixture of factual and fictional information. Actually, it was Abbot Laboratories (not Gerber) that was named in a lawsuit alleging baby-formula price-fixing from 1980 to 1992. The company agreed to pay rebates of $5 to $45; however, the recipients had to write to a post office box number in Minnesota to make their claim. In fact, it was the same post office box number on the Gerber fax I received.

At about the same time I got that fax, it was also making the rounds through the Chicago school system, where dozens of teachers and administrators were posting it on bulletin boards and sending copies of it home with students so mom and dad could get the rebate that was due. Meanwhile, some companies were inserting copies of the fax in employees' paycheck envelopes. This sort of thing was happening all over the country; at one point Gerber was receiving nearly 20,000 pieces of mail per month, and a similar number of phone inquiries, about the "big rebate."

The company remained remarkably calm through the run of this legend, which still crops up now and then. "We don't believe it's a scam. We think it's just misinformation," said a corporate spokesman

Gerber also posted an official response on its website:

The Classics

FREEMONT, MICH.—Gerber Products Company is not involved in any settlement involving reimbursements to consumers. Rumors that have been circulating for several months involving Gerber and an alleged settlement are completely false.

A settlement was announced in 1996 involving infant formula and pricing issues, but Gerber was not connected with the litigation. The deadline for filing claims under the infant formula settlement expired 1/31/97. It appears that the Gerber name has mistakenly been connected to the Minneapolis P.O. box used to process claims for the infant formula settlement. Gerber was advised by Minneapolis postal authorities that the P.O. box has been closed. It is our belief that the origin of this misinformation is the settlement announced in 1996 that involves infant formula.

It is unfortunate that consumers are being misled by this misinformation. Consumers are cautioned not to send birth records or other information connected with this rumor.

I would agree with Gerber's assertion that this is a myth borne mostly from good intentions. A few people got their facts screwed up and sincerely believed Gerber was offering a $500 rebate, and thousands of well-intentioned (if misinformed) people eagerly shared this news with friends and coworkers. But the company's suggested caution about sending birth records, e-mail addresses, social security numbers, and obviously cash, to unknown destinations is worth noting. As a spokesman for the Better Business Bureau told me, "If you give out that kind of information, you could become a victim of identity theft." In other words, some con artist can pretend to be you.

Look what happened to Sandra Bullock in *The Net*.

Craig Shergold's dying wish

Like a freckle-faced little boy in a long-running newspaper comic strip, Craig Shergold will never grow up. We won't let him. For the last decade, Craig has been "an eight-year-old boy suffering from terminal cancer," clinging to life while trying to fulfill his dream of making it into the *Guinness Book of World Records* for having the most business cards ever collected by a single individual.

That's where you come in. All you have to do is send your business card to a P.O. box set up by the Make-A-Wish Foundation (the wonderful organization that tries to make wishes come true for sick children), then pass along the message to all your friends and colleagues, and you can help this poor child achieve his goal before he succumbs to his illness.

Is there a company, a school, or civic organization in the world that hasn't received a chain letter about young Craig? (Sometimes his last name is "Sherford," or "Shelford," but his first name is almost always Craig.) Imagine hundreds upon hundreds of Girl Scout troops, Little League teams, Jaycees, Kiwanis, and well-meaning Fortune 500 companies all working hard to collect as many business cards as possible so they can put a smile on that kid's face. You can just see the teams of volunteers carefully packing yet another box of cards and sending it to the Foundation, where some warmhearted administrator will once again be moved by the outpouring of love and affection from those strangers touched by the plight of plucky young Craig Shergold.

Ah, but wipe those tears away, gentle reader, and focus on this: In the real world, if the Make-A-Wish people were granted a wish of their own, it would be that you would *stop sending all those damn business cards to them!*

Not that this is a fairy tale. Amazingly enough, there really is a Craig Shergold. He's from south London, and in 1989, at the age of ten, he was diagnosed as having a rare and terminal brain tumor. And he really did launch a drive to win a place in the *Guinness Book of World Records* by collecting cards—but they were greeting cards, not business cards.

If you check the mammoth 1999 Edition of the *Guinness Book of World Records*, you'll find that Craig achieved his goal.

Here's the best part of the story. In the spring of 1991, the billionaire John Kluge read about Craig's illness and arranged to have him brought to the University of Virginia Hospital. There, a team of skilled neurosurgeons removed nearly all of his tumor, which turned out to be benign. Craig is now in his late teens and in excellent heath.

As is the urban legend which bears his name. Somehow, a legitimate drive to collect greeting cards for Craig has morphed into an unstoppable beast of a chain letter. In 1994, the letter circulated through the offices of some of the most prominent business and Hollywood figures in the country, including Donald Trump, Mike Ovitz, Ted

Turner, Marvin Davis, and dozens of Fortune 500 CEOs. In 1998, a letter about the business card dreams of "Craig Sherford" made the rounds at newspapers such as the *Chicago Sun-Times*, the *Los Angeles Times* and the *San Francisco Examiner*, as well as the corporate offices of NBA Properties, NHL Enterprises and the Major League Baseball Players' Association. As usual, the mailing address was for the Make-A-Wish Foundation's branch in Atlanta.

Problem is, there is no office for Make-A-Wish in Atlanta. There *is* a Chicago office, however. When I called them to see if they could "clear up some confusion about this letter going around," the woman on the other end of the line said, "Craig Shergold! Would you please help us with this mess? It's driving us crazy." The Chicago office alone receives about a dozen calls a day on this subject—they've even set up a permanent message about Craig Shergold on their voice-mail system. (Call the national office at 1-800-722-9474 and they'll connect you to the message.) Said Steve Cohen, national president of Make-A-Wish: "Our office continues to receive thousands of phone calls [about Craig Shergold] every month, diverting our staff time and resources from our mission."

In other words, the time wasted on this urban legend could be devoted to helping little Johnny or little Mindy get to Disney World. Mention that the next time some clown comes to you with a plea to help perpetually eight-year-old Craig gather the world's largest collection of business cards.

"Are you Gay?"

Provided the flight isn't completely booked, airline employees are often allowed to hitch a free ride on their company's planes. It's one of the perks of the job. An employee for USAir—a man who happened to have the last name of Gay—boarded a plane on one of these free-flight deals, but when he arrived at his assigned seat, another passenger was already settled in. Not wanting to cause any problems, Mr. Gay took a different seat.

What Mr. Gay didn't know was that another USAir carrier heading for his destination was experiencing technical problems, which resulted in the cancellation of that particular flight. The passengers on this other flight were being rerouted to Mr. Gay's gate, meaning that the flight was now overbooked, and according to company regulations, he would have to be bumped from the flight in favor of a paying customer.

A flight attendant was given a list containing the names of a handful of passengers who were USAir employees and thus would have to exit the plane. (As you'll recall, Mr. Gay was not sitting in his assigned seat, which had been swiped by an unwitting passenger.) The flight attendant approached the passenger in Mr. Gay's seat and said in a loud voice: "Are you Gay?"

"Excuse me?" said the startled man, as his fellow passengers looked on in amazement.

"We don't have time to argue about this, are you Gay or not?" the flight attendant demanded.

"No!" the man proclaimed.

The flight attendant looked again at her list. "Come on! Are you sure you're not Gay?"

"I don't know what you're talking about," said the man, who was growing ever more flustered.

"I'm going to ask you this one last time before we have a major problem," said the flight attendant. "Are you or are you not Gay?"

At this point the man slumped in his seat and said in a soft voice, "All right, all right. Yes I am. I'm gay."

"Then you have to get off the plane. Let's go," said the flight attendant, grabbing the poor man by the arm.

By this time, the *real* Mr. Gay had become aware of the situation, so he leaped to his feet and said, "You've got the wrong man! I'm Gay!"

With that, a man sitting a few rows back jumped up and said, "I'm gay too, and damn proud of it! What are they going to do, throw us all off the plane? This is discrimination!"

Caught up in the moment, a number of other passengers began to make a ruckus, demanding that all gays be allowed to fly on USAir without fear of discrimination. The poor flight attendant burst into tears while the pilot radioed for security to storm the plane and take control of the situation. When the dust had finally settled, the first gay passenger had been given a pass good for free travel on USAir for an entire year, and the flight attendant was sent home to recover from the traumatic situation. As for Mr. Gay, he quit USAir and found a job with another airline.

This story has supposedly appeared in a number of gay and lesbian publications, but I was unable to find one example of any organization taking it seriously. (Maybe it was inspired by the scene at the end of *In and Out*, where dozens of individuals, including crusty old Wilford Brimley, stand up during the graduation ceremony to proclaim "I'm gay!")

A spokesperson for USAir said, "Of course we have zero tolerance for any kind of discrimination," but added that he'd need specific information (the date of the incident, flight number, etc.) to check into the story. Naturally, I couldn't provide him with such information because there was no such incident.

Why is USAir almost always the airline named in this story? It's not because they have any record of discrimination against gays. Most likely, the airline was mentioned in an early, anonymous fax or Internet posting by some disgruntled employee who thought it would tarnish the company's image.

Laptop dangers

I've seen all those statistics proving that flying on a commercial airline is much safer than driving a car or shooting yourself in the head, but I still get a little worried when I fly—especially when they ask everyone to "turn off all electronic and recording devices." What? My Sony Walkman or little Game Boy can crash a plane? I don't want to hear that!

Likewise, I'm always a bit fearful I'll get into trouble when I turn on my laptop computer. I envision the flight attendants rushing down the aisle as warning lights flash, buzzers ring, and babies start to cry as we lose altitude. *Stop him before he reboots again!*

There are horror stories about people who have seen their computers melt down on flights. See, some international carriers have tray tables laced with magnetic strips; the strips are there so that when you place your tray table in the armrest, it doesn't jiggle around and create a lot of noise. The problem is, the airlines never tell you about this. Unwitting travelers go through their usual routines of placing their laptops on the tables, only to see their hard drives mysteriously corrupted by the magnetized trays. The airlines know what's happening, but they're not going to make it public because they'd be liable for damages. What they've been doing is quietly replacing the magnetized trays with good old-fashioned plastic models. No doubt somebody lost their job over this mess, but so far, the airlines have been able to avoid the negative publicity that would surely be generated if the secret got out.

That's how the myth was told to me in 1998. Some Internet postings even mention a particular airline—Delta-owned Sabena Belgium World—as having the magnetized trays. Supposedly, the new Airbus 340 planes were outfitted with magnetized trays that have been crashing hard drives. The postings advise travelers to place a paper clip on their trays to test them out before turning on their laptops.

This rumor continues to make the rounds, even though it has no basis in fact. "It is indeed a myth," said Betty Moore of Delta's corporate communications staff. "Our trays have no effect on laptop computers."

No airline has ever used magnetized trays—and as long as you've got an okay from the flight crew to turn on your computer, there's nothing to worry about.

Just be careful with that hand-held Game Boy. Lives are at stake!

Y2K's extra day

By the time you read this, I'll be safely ensconced in my soundproof, bulletproof, bombproof shelter, where I plan to wait out the madness as the millennium bug known as Y2K takes over the world, causing plane crashes, banking nightmares, elevator disasters, water shortages and the sort of general chaos not seen since the Mets won the World Series. You'll be scrambling for your lives, you ill-prepared non-believers, but I'll be living the good life in my cinderblock lair, wearing my camouflage outfit, drinking bottled water, eating powdered eggs, and triple-checking the locks to make sure nobody can get in. It'll be Utopia!

All right, so I'm not really doing that, but some people are. They call themselves "survivalists." I call them something else. I'm not saying there won't be any computer glitches because of the Y2K bug, but the idea that the world will come to a crashing end because the Gregorian calendar clicks over from 1999 to 2000 is insane. (Should I even bother pointing out that the next millennium doesn't really begin until Jan. 1, 2001? Probably not. The math is too confusing for a world in which our cash registers and calculators do all the work for us.

In February of 1999, I was told something new about the year 2000. Turns out it's a rare "double leap year," something that occurs only every 400 years. That means February, 2000, will have not 28 days, not 29 days, but 30 days. In other words, the year 2000 will have 367 days!

Now, time is not perfect. More accurately, our method of measuring time is not perfect, so each day extends a few extra seconds beyond the 24-hour mark. Every four years, we add an extra day in February to "soak up" all those accumulated seconds, and that keeps the calendar accurate. But the leap day itself contains a few extra seconds, and so every 400 years we have to add an *extra* extra day. The last time that happened was in 1600, and it's going to occur again in 2000.

Technically speaking, if you're born on Feb. 29 you can truly celebrate only once every four years. Consider the child who comes into the world on Feb. 30, 2000. He or she will never have a real birthday, because the next Feb. 30 won't occur until the year 2400. And unless we make some serious gains in medicine and science, the average life span isn't likely to hit the 400-year mark any time soon.

But the added day isn't just a charming quirk—it's also a new concern for computer programmers. Just as most computers weren't built to accept the year 2000, they have nothing in their systems to accommodate a Feb. 30. Even computers with built-in leap year applications only recognize Feb. 29. On 2/29/00, those computers will operate correctly, but on 2/30/00, there's not a computer in the world that will accept that date. They'll all be saying it's March 1.

It's going to be a nightmare. If you think Y2K is all about New Year's Day, think again. Feb. 30, 2000, is another potential rendezvous with catastrophe.

Not to worry. The "super leap year" does not exist. It's either the product of a hoaxter's imagination, or a misunderstanding about how leap years work. According to our modern calendar, any year that's divisible by four is a leap year, with the exception of years ending in 00. So 1896 and 1904 were leap years, but the year 1900 was not.

However, a year ending in 00 *is* a leap year if it's also divisible by 400. That means 1900, 1800 and 1700 were not leap years, but 1600 was, and 2000 will be. The number 2000 is evenly divisible by 400, so the rule applies. We will have a Feb. 29, 2000, but there won't be a Feb. 30. There never has been, not even in years divisible by 400.

If your brain hurts trying to compute all these numbers, don't worry. The people who make wall calendars and date minders know all this stuff and they won't let us down.

Earthquake squashes car thief

If your car has ever been stolen or vandalized—the window smashed, the radio ripped from its moorings, the change you keep for the toll booth gone—you know what it's like to feel a thirst for revenge. You want the cops to catch the bum, and the courts to put him away for a long, long time. You might even fantasize about what it would have been like to happen upon the creep while he was in the middle of defiling your vehicle.

Once in a while we hear about a car thief who is punished severely for his sins—perhaps even beyond what he deserves. While none of us wishes death or serious injury on car thieves, it's not as if there's a great outcry of public sympathy when such an accident occurs.

One story about a car thief really catching a karmic boomerang supposedly occurred during the disastrous San Francisco earthquake of October 17, 1989.

A childhood friend who has lived in the Bay Area since college was the first to tell me the story, which he believed to be absolutely true. It seemed that his girlfriend's coworker's sister and brother-in-law had driven their new BMW to Candlestick Park on October 17 for the third World Series game. You might recall that before the game could be played, serious tremors rocked the ballpark, and the game subsequently was canceled as everyone scrambled for the parking lot.

The understandably shaken young couple wandered around the lot, trying to remember where they'd parked their new car, when a sickening thought hit the husband.

"We're not going to find the car," he told his wife.

"What are you talking about, of course we're going to find it," she said. "Now is not the time to panic!"

"You don't understand," the husband said. "We're not going to find the car because it's been stolen. I wrote where we parked on the back of the ticket stub, and that's the spot right there."

The husband and wife walked for quite a while before finally managing to catch a cab home, which fortunately was not in an area hit by the earthquake. When they arrived home, they called the police and filed a report, but a stolen car was obviously a low priority in the midst of such a disaster.

Several days later, the San Francisco police called to say the BMW had been found on the I-880 freeway.

"What kind of condition is it in?" the young woman asked.

"What kind of condition is it in?" repeated the police officer. "Are you kidding me? It was found by a construction crew excavating the freeway, ma'am. It's flatter than a Frisbee."

"Oh, I feel awful," said the young woman.

"Not as bad as the thief must have felt," replied the cop. "He was in the car when they found it."

"You mean the guy who stole our car is dead?"

"Flatter than a Frisbee, too, ma'am."

⬚ ⬚ ⬚

I've heard variations on this story. Sometimes the car is a Mercedes, a Porsche, or a Land Rover instead of a BMW; sometimes it's found on the Nimitz Freeway, or in a collapsed parking lot, or beneath the rubble of a building that was felled by the quake. In particularly imaginative variations, the police don't just phone the news to the couple, they show up at their home with a crushed steering wheel or license plate.

A spokesman for the San Francisco Police Department told me he'd never heard the story, "but that doesn't mean it couldn't have happened."

True enough. But if it had happened, you'd think there would have been a few dozen reports about it. Judy Canter, head librarian for the *San Francisco Examiner*, researched the paper's archives and found nothing about a car thief being killed in the 1989 quake.

"Good luck, Mr. Gorsky"

When Apollo 11 astronaut Neil Armstrong set foot on the moon, he fumbled one of the most famous lines of the 20th century. The plan was for Armstrong to say, "That's one small step for a man, one giant leap for mankind," a poetic statement that would have downplayed the individual glory of the feat and emphasized the victory achieved by all humanity. But Armstrong dropped the "a" from in front of the word "man," which rendered his proclamation essentially meaningless. To say "One small step for man, one giant leap for mankind" is to utter a redundancy, as in this context, "man" and "mankind" are the same thing.

Perhaps it is this gaffe that gave rise to the common belief that Armstrong issued a second and even more cryptic message as he began to leave footprints in the moondust.

After the "one small step" comment, the communication line between NASA's Mission Control and Armstrong remained open, and they engaged in scientific small talk as he walked on the moon. At one point Armstrong uttered the mysterious line, "Good luck, Mr. Gorsky," prompting the gang at Mission Control to ask Armstrong for a clarification of the statement. He pretended not to know what they were talking about, and for years afterward, Armstrong feigned ignorance.

Many observers figured Armstrong was addressing a Soviet cosmonaut named Gorsky, but a records check of all Russians involved in that country's space program turns up no one with that name. Others thought Armstrong was making a personal reference to a friend.

In a way, that theory would be correct. Nearly three decades after he landed on the moon, Armstrong finally revealed the answer to this mystery at a press conference in Florida, when a young reporter who had studied grainy old footage of the historic moment asked the legendary astronaut about the infamous Mr. Gorsky.

Grinning slyly, Armstrong said, "Ah, what the hell. Now that Mr. Gorsky has passed away, I don't think there's any harm in telling the story. And I doubt the brass at NASA can do anything after all these years!"

It seems that when Armstrong was a boy of 10 or 11, he lived next door to a middle-aged couple, the Gorskys. One day, the neighborhood kids were playing baseball in Armstrong's backyard when young Neil hit the ball into the next yard, where it bounced around before coming to rest just beneath the Gorskys' bedroom window. Neil climbed the fence and scampered over to retrieve the ball—and that's when he heard the argument between Mr. and Mrs. Gorsky.

"You want oral sex?" Mrs. Gorsky said with a laugh. "I'll tell you what. You'll get oral sex when the kid next door walks on the moon!"

Many years later, as he took that historic walk on the moon, Neil Armstrong thought of that long-ago promise and, in typically cheeky astronaut fashion, couldn't resist sending a message of good luck to old Mr. Gorsky.

⊠ ⊠ ⊠

Funny story? Phony story. Study footage of the Apollo 11 moon landing, listen closely to the dialogue, and you'll hear nothing that even remotely resembles a reference to any "Gorsky." A Nexis search yielded hundreds of stories about Neil Armstrong, but nothing about any Florida press conference where the so-called secret was revealed.

Brian Welch, director of media services for NASA, told me, "We've heard that [story], and it never happened. I've gotten several inquiries about it. It struck me as a 'Yeah, sure' story, but I still had the Johnson Space Center scan the transcripts from Apollo 11. There's nothing like that in the transcripts."

Just to triple-check, I studied the transcripts myself. After Armstrong said, "That's one small step for man, one giant leap for mankind," there was a pause of about 30 seconds as he began walking on the moon. His next comment was, "The surface is fine and powdery. I can kick it up loosely with my toe. It does adhere in fine layers, like powdered charcoal, to the sole and sides of my boots. I only go in a small fraction of an inch, maybe an eighth of an inch, but I can see the footprints of my boots and treads in fine, sandy particles."

And so on. I studied pages and pages of transcripts, but there's nothing about a Mr. Gorsky. Armstrong never even says anything like, "I'm on the moon and you're not!"

That's one small step backward for an urban legend, one giant leap for mankind.

UL FOOTNOTE. Another NASA-related bit of folklore has to do with the science teacher who was "runner-up" to Christa McAuliffe, the schoolteacher who was killed in the *Challenger* explosion. Thousands of instructors applied to become the first teacher in space, but there was never any official second place finisher in the competition. Nevertheless, you'll often see postings like this one on the Internet:

"I have met at least five people who *swear* that back when the *Challenger* had its fateful flight, *their* teacher was the first runner-up to Christa McAuliff (*sic*), the first teacher in space, who blew up with the Challenger. It's always told as a parable about how sometimes losing is really a blessing. So were there just a ton of teachers who were told they were runners-up?"

Answer: No.

Exploding flashlights

You can imagine this UL as the opening scene in an action thriller, maybe *Lethal Weapon 17: The Golden Years*, starring Mel Gibson and Danny Glover, and their false teeth.

A small bomb has gone off in a building after business hours, and now the cops are on the scene, sifting through the rubble in the darkness. One investigator finds a flashlight, and he flicks it on—triggering another explosion that kills several officers. The device had been booby-trapped by a cop-hating killer.

Except it's not a movie, it's really happening. Or so we're led to believe by the warning that has circulated through police stations and posted on more than a few workplace bulletin boards. It starts off with a lot of official-looking text, but the phrasing itself is laughable, as if a 12-year-old prank artist somewhere was trying hard to sound like a government official.

SUBJECT: Safety Alert—Secondary Explosive Devices

SOURCE: HQ Naval Criminal Investigative Services (NCIS), Washington, D.C.

SUMMARY. There has been a recent increase in the use of flashlights as housings for explosive devices in the United States and its territories. Essentially, individuals have been booby trapping flashlights and leaving them at crime scenes and bomb and arson scenes. To date, these devices have killed one law enforcement officer and have injured several officers and several civilians. The flashlights are generally metal. The batteries are removed and a small pipe bomb is inserted into the housing. The bomber then rigs the flashlight in one of two ways—either wiring the flashlight to explode when the switch is activated, or setting the bomb to trigger if the device is moved at all. A mag light rigged with an improvised motion switch claimed the life of a Puerto Rican peace officer.

During any crime scene investigation, if a flashlight is discovered, leave said light *alone*. If the owner of the flashlight is discovered, allow the owner to take custody of the flashlight. If no owner can be found, contact the local bomb squad *immediately*. If the bomb squad tries to laugh you off, remind them that ATF has reported finding about 20 of these flashlight bombs in the last year and tell them you're not going to touch it.

If this makes you nervous or apprehensive, good. If you are nervous and apprehensive about things that you find, then you'll be careful and get home alive with all of your various body parts intact.

SUGGESTED ACTIONS. Share this information with Commanders, First Sergeants, Security Forces and local law enforcement agencies.

I love the part about what to do "if the bomb squad tries to laugh you off." And what's with the "Puerto Rican peace officer?" Is that a lame attempt to give the "warning" extra import so it'll seem more authentic?

Is it possible to place an explosive device in a flashlight? Absolutely. All manners of cylindrical devices can be used to house small pipe bombs. Jerry Singer, a special agent with the Chicago Field Division of the Bureau of Alcohol, Tobacco and Firearms told me, "We don't take anything for granted. Any time agents arrive on a bomb scene, they enter very cautiously, making certain the scene is structurally and environmentally safe, and that there is not a second explosive device present. I've never heard of exploding flashlights."

Until they make *Lethal Weapon 17*, that is.

The toothbrush bandits

After a lavish wedding paid for by their affluent families, a lovely young bride and her groom head from New York to Jamaica for a fabulous honeymoon in a posh resort. For several days they live in a dream world of sumptuous meals, champagne toasts, midnight walks on the beach, and great sex.

"This is the perfect honeymoon," says the bride as she and her new husband head back to their hotel room after another great day on the beach. But when they arrive at their room, they discover that thieves have broken in and cleaned the place out, taking nearly everything that wasn't nailed down. Their clothes, their jewelry, the souvenirs they'd purchased—all gone.

"They've taken everything!" the groom says as he goes from room to room and closet to closet.

"Well, almost everything," says the tearful bride as she emerges from the bathroom. "I guess they didn't have any need for our toothbrushes—and look on the floor by the nightstand. They left our camera."

The police are summoned and reports are filled out, but the newlyweds know they'll never get their stuff back, nor will their insurance cover the sentimental value of some of the stolen items. They consider cutting short the honeymoon, but why let the theft ruin their vacation? With the help of their credit card company, they're able to get enough cash and credit to buy new clothes and supplies so they can continue with their special romantic holiday, which concludes without further incident.

A week later, they're back in New York when the bride calls her husband at work to tell him the honeymoon shots are back from the photo lab.

"Why don't we have a few friends over for drinks tonight and we'll go through the pictures?" she says, and her husband readily agrees. That night, they're flipping through the photos with a half-dozen of their closest friends who are at least pretending to be interested. Suddenly the room grows quiet when the bride comes across several pictures of...

"Those look like two butts!" squeals one of the guests. "And judging by all the hair on them, I'd say they're male butts."

"I don't understand," says the bride. "Who took this picture? What's it doing with our honeymoon photos? And what are those, those, *things* sticking out of them?"

· "Oh my God," says the groom. "Those are our toothbrushes!"

The bride races to the bathroom and slams the door—and there are the toothbrushes in question, taunting her by their very presence. She barely makes it to the toilet in time before furiously upchucking.

☒ ☒ ☒

The legend of the Toothbrush Bandits has been told so often I'm surprised some real thieves haven't tried the trick by now, as a tribute to this gross but pretty funny story. This is one UL I believed to be absolutely true when I first heard it in the early 1990s. Because of the gross-out factor involved in this story, it's a particular favorite of teenagers.

In the meantime, let's consider some of the factors that make this story so unlikely.

Supposedly, this tale has taken place in the Bahamas, Jamaica, Acapulco, the Cayman Islands, Hawaii, Cozumel, Las Vegas—in short, nearly every place an American couple might choose as a honeymoon destination. That's an awful lot of toothbrushes going into an awful lot of rear ends!

Also, for the story to achieve maximum gross-out potential, the toothbrushes must be inserted bristles-first. I suppose there might be a team of practical joke-loving, exhibitionist, anal-masochist bandits with toothbrush fetishes out there—but then again, maybe not.

You'd also think a honeymooning couple would take their camera with them in order to capture the memories of a lifetime—or, upon returning to the room and inspecting the camera, they'd notice that the counter had advanced several numbers, indicating that someone had used it. Barring that, would the average photo lab even develop such pictures?

UL FOOTNOTE. David Foster Wallace's dense novel *Infinite Jest* features a variation of the toothbrush-bandit story. In the book, a burglar named Don Gately and his partner break into the home of the assistant District Attorney who had put Gately away, and they steal "a coin collection and two antique shotguns." A month later, the attorney receives an envelope containing "two high-pixel Polaroid snapshots, one of big Don Gately and one of his associate, each in a Halloween mask denoting a clown's great good professional cheer, each with his pants down and bent over and each with the handle of one of the couple's toothbrushes protruding from his bottom."

Now where in the world would the novelist come up with an anecdote like that?

Legends
of
Rolling Rock

One of the best (and one of the worst) things about drinking beer is that it makes matters of niggling significance take on added importance.

Such as label fascination.

The more beers you consume, the more interested you become in the can or bottle on the table in front of you. Look at that marvelously ornate design and the exquisite detail of the Budweiser logo. What's the significance of the various creatures and humans on the Old Style can? Turn this empty bottle of Red Dog upside down, and watch how the dog's face turns into the image of a man and woman engaged in an intimate act.

Those were not random examples. I've actually had deep and meaningful conversations about each of the above topics. (And people ask why I've never been married.) Some breweries are quite hip to this label-fascination thing. For example, take a look at bottles of Miller Genuine Draft, which have bizarre and provocative black-and-white photos on the insides of the labels, which means they come into focus only after you've downed most of the product. What purpose do those photos serve other than to arouse the curiosity of the Miller drinker and entice him or her to order another to see if a different image appears on the inside.

For sheer intrigue, however, nothing matches the long-running speculation about the mysterious "33" that appears on every can and bottle of Rolling Rock beer. It's the stuff of, well, urban legend.

Rolling Rock is brewed in Latrobe, Pennsylvania, a town of about 12,000 situated at the foothills of the Allegheny Mountains. The Latrobe Brewing Company was founded in the late 19th century, was forced to close during Prohibition, and reopened in 1933.

That's it! The brewery reopened in '33, hence the "33" on the labels. At least, that's one explanation you'll hear in barrooms, but it's one of the numerous incorrect theories.

I've also heard that 33 is the number of days between the time a batch is brewed and the time it's bottled. Wrong again.

Does the "33" represent the number of bottles consumed by a legendary bear of a man in western Pennsylvania who celebrated the end of Prohibition by drinking until he nearly died of alcohol consumption?

Is 33 the number of German monks who settled in Latrobe in the 1890s and sold their recipe for beer to the brewery's founders?

Do 33 employees have a hand in the making of each bottle of Rolling Rock? Is the current version of the beer made with the 33rd version of the original recipe?

No, no, no, and no again.

Even the best and most plausible explanation cannot be confirmed, because the makers of Rolling Rock figured out long ago that mystery sells better than reality. (If you call Latrobe headquarters at 724-537-5546, you can hear "theories about the mystical '33' " by pressing 9. But they don't provide the definitive explanation.)

Nonetheless, we offer the following as the best theory.

Beer drinkers are, for the most part, regular working stiffs devoid of pretense, but for some reason breweries like to pretend they're as snooty and sophisticated as the owners of the world's finest vineyards. Whether we're talking microbrew or mass-produced swill, the cans and bottles will often include some sort of company motto or pledge, along with a short history of the brewery.

And so it is with Rolling Rock. In the late 1930s, they were trying to come up with a mission statement to be painted onto each green glass bottle, and somebody penned the words you still see on every can or bottle to leave the brewery:

Rolling Rock
From the glass lined tanks of Old Latrobe
We tender this premium beer for your enjoyment,
As a tribute to your good taste
It comes from the mountain springs to you
"33"

Take a moment to count the number of words in that pledge. That's right: 33.

But why would they want us to know this number? According to company lore, it was a mistake. Whoever wrote the pledge jotted down "33" to let his bosses know how many words were in the message, and somebody mistakenly included the number in the final design. The company saw no need to destroy thousands of otherwise perfectly good bottles, so they let the error go—and when they saw how the "33" caught on with the drinking public, they decided to make it a permanent part of the logo design.

In a 1997 feature in the *Pittsburgh Tribune-Review*, a number of Rolling Rock managers were asked about the 33 legend, but they all good-naturedly refused to answer—although one fellow did say, "People have guessed the answer. It's out there."

Growing up in Chicago, I'd never even heard of Rolling Rock until I saw *The Deer Hunter*, in which Pennsylvania boys Robert DeNiro, John Savage and Christopher Walken gush about Rolling Rock at the wedding reception at the beginning of the movie. Since then I've consumed at least a six-pack of Rolling Rock. Maybe even a few more than that.

Hey, if it's good enough for DeNiro, it's good enough for me.

"Welcome to the world of AIDS"

Other diseases will kill you just as dead, but AIDS is the scariest illness of our times. When the AIDS out break hit the United States in the mid-1980s, a flood of misinformation washed over the populace, which gave rise to myriad stories and myths about how one might "catch" the virus. To this day you'll run into ignorant fools who will insist you can get AIDS from a mosquito bite, a kiss, even a toilet seat. (I guess the worst-case scenario would be if you were sitting on a toilet seat in a public restroom, exchanging an open-mouthed kiss with someone while a mosquito bites you.) Though these claims have no basis in medical reality, try telling that to the fearmongers.

Admittedly, there have been a number of bizarre and horrific real-life stories of "innocent" people who have been infected or were threatened with infection via unconventional and nefarious means, and that has only added credibility to the bogus stories. In Florida, an HIV-positive dentist transmitted the virus to several of his patients. Police officers and health care workers have been put at risk by someone with AIDS spitting at them or biting them. The late Elizabeth Glaser, wife of actor Paul

Michael Glaser, contracted the virus through a blood transfusion, as did tennis great Arthur Ashe. Though the risk of infection from such scenarios is minuscule, it adds fuel to the claims that you can "catch" AIDS from all sorts of sources.

The fact is, if you don't engage in any high-risk activities such as unprotected sex with multiple strangers or shooting up with a dirty needle, chances are quite good you won't get AIDS; however, there's still that minute but very real possibility you could be victimized by a freak accident or a freaky human. This irrational fear has spawned a number of AIDS-related urban legends, including the widespread tale of the innocent moviegoer who feels a slight pinprick on her leg or back, followed by itching and bleeding; when she examines the wound, she sees that someone has left a sticker on her proclaiming WELCOME TO THE WORLD OF AIDS. She figures it's just a sick practical joke, until a blood test a few weeks later reveals she's HIV-positive.

"Be careful the next time you go to a cinema," reads a typical warning posted on the Internet. "These people could be anywhere! [This really happened] to a friend of my brother's wife."

Why is it that the teller of the urban legend is always at least two steps removed from the principal in the story? Wouldn't it be refreshing to hear from someone who says, "I know the guy this happened to—it's me! And I have video documentation and medical and police records to back up my story. In fact, I'll be on *Nightline* next Tuesday to tell the whole tale! Make sure you tune in."

Even more popular than the needle-jabbing tale is the UL about the one-night stand gone wrong.

A young woman is devastated after her fiance calls off their wedding just days in advance. She decides to go on the honeymoon to Jamaica by herself to drown her sorrows. On her final night of vacation, she gets really drunk with a handsome stranger, and they begin to kiss in the bar.

"Spend the night with me," he says. "I know it's sudden, and I know you're not the kind of girl who would normally do something like this, but I have to get on a plane to New York in the morning, and I don't know if I'm ever going to see you again."

She's not herself. The shock from the broken engagement, the pain she's feeling inside, the liquor swirling inside her...in that moment she makes a decision she never would have dreamed of making just a few weeks earlier. She brings him back to the hotel room (where she was supposed to be spending her honeymoon) for a night of wild, carefree, unconventional sex. Never before has she felt so free, so unbridled. She does things with this stranger she never even thought about doing with her ex-fiance.

In the morning, the woman wakes up alone. She's got a pounding headache from all the drinks and feels a bit guilty about what she did, but she can't help but smile when she replays the great sex of the night before. She rolls over and reaches across the bed, but the stranger is long gone.

No matter. It was just a one-night thing, and well worth it. She feels as if she can go back home and get on with her life.

Just then, the phone rings. It's her former fiance, calling from the airport back home. He's so glad he tracked her down before she got on a plane, because he wants to join her and make things right. Spending time away from her has convinced him that he made the biggest mistake of his life, and now all he wants to do is make it up to her. If only she'll let him come down, he's sure they can patch things up. They can even get married right there in the tropical paradise.

They talk on the phone for an hour and a half. Finally the young woman allows herself to admit she still loves him. She tells him to get on the next plane for Jamaica.

After she hangs up, she feels a sharp pang of remorse about the previous night's activities. Even though the relationship with her fiance was technically at an impasse, she feels as if she's betrayed him. But who's ever going to know what happened?

She walks into the bathroom and starts the shower. As she's slipping off her robe she glances at the mirror—and her blood-curdling cry of horror can be heard throughout the hotel. Seems her one-night lover had left behind a message, scrawled with her own lipstick on the mirror: WELCOME TO THE WORLD OF AIDS.

☒ ☒ ☒

Before the AIDS era, this same story was told often, but then the message on the mirror was WELCOME TO THE WORLD OF SYPHILIS. Wasn't true then, either.

The Center for Disease Control in Atlanta has never been informed of a documented incident of someone getting AIDS from a one-night stand with a seductive sicko.

"There has never been a case like this reported to the CDC," said Kitty Bina, HIV media specialist for the Center. "There is no documentation of such a case." Bina added that if something like that did occur, it wouldn't *have* to be reported to the CDC, but an extensive review of newspaper and magazine articles yielded no documentation either, even though the story has made the rounds of nearly every major city in the country.

Bozo
no-no

When I was a kid growing up outside Chicago in the 1960s and 1970s, there was no tougher ticket in town than *Bozo's Circus*, a daily, one-hour, locally produced program featuring host Ringmaster Ned and a cadre of clowns including Cookie, Oliver O. Oliver, and the immortal Bozo. A live audience packed the bleachers each day to watch skits, cartoons, circus acts, and bands.

Bozo's Circus was the hottest show in town. Couples that didn't even have children would get their names on the waiting list. It was not unheard of to wait three or four years for tickets to see Bozo. The highlight of each show was the "Grand Prize Game," in which two tykes would be selected from the audience to throw Ping-Pong balls into six buckets one at a time. The farther away the bucket, the more difficult the shot and the better the prize.

You kept going until you missed, which usually happened by the third or fourth bucket. Ringmaster Ned would drop a silver dollar in Bucket #6 each day until somebody finally made the shot, at which point the crowd would go wild, the kid would get all the silver dollars, and Bozo would come out riding the "Grand Prize": a new bicycle.

As kids, we thought *Bozo's Circus* was unique to Chicago, but dozens of cities had their own version of the circus, just like they had their own local *Romper Room* in the morning. And that's why people all over the country are absolutely sure they witnessed the moment when Bozo got his comeuppance from a smart-aleck kid who had bombed out on the Grand Prize Game.

Seems there was this little troublemaker who was selected to participate in the Grand Prize Game. He was thrilled to make the first two buckets, but when toss number three bounced off the rim, he blurted, "Oh, hell!"

The crowd of moms and dads and little kids was stunned silent. Ringmaster Ned didn't know what to say. Clowns and jugglers looked on from the wings in open-mouthed shock. Finally Bozo stepped forward and said, "Now, now, little boy, that's a Bozo no-no."

"Ah, cram it, clownie!" said the boy as he stomped off. They cut to a commercial, and when the show returned, Bozo and Ringmaster Ned gave a talk about curse words and why they're not for children.

A friend of mine who grew up in Baltimore "remembered" the story a bit differently. "There was a game where you had to walk across the room with an egg on a spoon, and if your egg dropped, you were eliminated," she told me. "When this little boy's egg fell off the spoon, he started to cry, so Bozo rushed over and gave him some kind of cheap consolation prize, like a T-shirt or something, and the kid looked up at Bozo and said, 'Why don't you shove your stupid toy, Bozo.' "

The clown in question isn't always named Bozo, either. In some cities they had knockoff versions of *Bozo's Circus*, with the lead clown named Chuckles, or Shakes, or Gary, or whatever. Weirdly enough, Larry Harmon, who was the original Bozo and is credited with creating the Bozo franchise, has bought into this urban legend. According to Harmon, it really happened in Boston in the 1960s, though he doesn't have any more evidence than anyone else.

That the story has been told so many times in so many cities is the best evidence that it never happened. However, *Bozo's Circus* was almost always televised live, so it's possible that at some point in some city, some little kid mixed it up with Bozo and uttered an expletive or two. But you'd think such an incident would have at least merited a mention in a local paper somewhere. No such stories have ever been unearthed.

So the next time someone swears to have seen the show in question, remind them that trying to pass off urban legends as fact is a Bozo no-no.

Chapter Two
Big Lies
on Campus

It made sense for the movie *Urban Legend* to take place in and around a college campus, as these institutions of higher learning have long been fertile ground for the launching and retelling of literally dozens of modern myths, most of them covering one of three topics: murder, sex, or cheating on exams.

A college campus is the perfect place for a too-good-to-be-true story to thrive for generations. With a complete turnover of the student population every four or five years, the tale can be passed from one class to another, and in dorm rooms, fraternity, and sorority houses, with the original source long since removed. Many of these stories sound quite plausible, if it weren't for the fact that the same elements of a story will crop up in campuses across the country...

Psychic predicts massacre

If somebody at Bowling Green State University in Ohio had talked to somebody at the University of San Diego in California in October of 1998, both schools could have avoided a lot of unnecessary panic. Based on the stories sweeping their respective campuses at the time, a conversation between our imaginary students might have gone something like this:

Bowling Green Student: "You're never going to believe what's happening here! People are freaking out."

San Diego Student: "You think you're freaking out there, you should see what's going on here! I guarantee you it's crazier than anything happening on your campus. We're in the middle of a major meltdown, I know you can't top that."

BG: "I wouldn't be so sure. It's insane around here."

SD: "OK, I'll go first and then you can tell me your story. There's this psychic guy—he's supposed to be the most famous psychic in the world, he predicted the Oklahoma City bombing—and he went on Oprah Winfrey's show and predicted there was going to be a mass murder on Halloween at an H-shaped residence hall, and guess what, *we* have an H-shaped residence hall at USD...well actually, it's more of an A-shape, but it's close enough, and it's called Camino/Founders Hall, so everybody who lives there is totally losing it and—"

BG: "Wait a min—"

SD: "Hold on. This psychic predicted the massacre would take place on Halloween, and everybody on campus has been talking about it and people are getting really scared, and there's something like 280 women who live in Camino/Founders Hall and everyone who lives there is clearing out. Camino/Founders is a total ghost town right now."

(There's a long pause)

SD: "What's the matter?"

BG: "I don't know what you're talking about, because the psychic who was on *Oprah* didn't say anything about an H-shaped building. He said the massacre was going to take place at a state college in the Midwest and he even mentioned Bowling Green as one of the possibilities, and that's why people are freaking out here!"

SD: "I don't get it. Did you see the show when the guy was on?"

BG: "Um, no. Did you?"

SD: "No, I didn't see it either. What's going on here?"

$$\boxtimes \quad \boxtimes \quad \boxtimes$$

The reason neither of our mythological students saw the psychic's appearance is that there has never been such a segment of *Oprah*.

Sure, Oprah's been doing some bizarre shows in the last few years, but as of this writing, she has yet to sink to such depths as allowing on a psychic to predict a mass murder on a college campus. And it's a pretty safe bet she never will.

Nevertheless, the feelings of fear on the campuses of the University of San Diego and Bowling Green State University in the fall of 1998 were very palpable. A story published on Oct. 31 in the *San Diego Union-Tribune* said that "most residents [of Camino/Founders Hall] were looking for somewhere else to spend the weekend" due to the spreading of a "classic urban legend." The resident assistants at the dorm said efforts to calm students were largely futile, with one RA saying only four of the 37 women she supervised planned to stay in their dorms Halloween night—"and they've all decided to hang out with me."

The paper quoted one student who spoke with great authority about the danger facing dorm residents: "The psychic predicted that there would be a mass murder at a Southern California school with an H-shaped dorm like ours. They did some research about H-shaped dorms, and only a couple of schools in the nation have them."

On the very same day, more than halfway across the country, a similar story attempting to diffuse the legend appeared in the *Columbus* (Ohio) *Dispatch*. In this version, the killer was supposedly going to be dressed like a clown—an evil killer clown. A veteran official at the university said the story was so familiar to longtime employees that "we may even have a file on this one." Some students had heard the killer would be wearing a Little Bo Peep costume.

Meanwhile, similar rumors circulated through the University of Michigan, Kent State University, the University of Iowa, and the University of Illinois. Patient spokespeople for Oprah's show explained again that nothing even remotely resembling such an incident had ever happened. (According to another rumor, the prediction had occurred and the show was taped but it never aired. Oprah supposedly told her studio audience she'd never let the segment see the light of day, but word leaked anyway.)

Students at San Diego, Bowling Green, et al., soon realized the scare was borne of pure fiction, but that certainly won't stop the Class of '00 or later from going through the whole thing again. The psychic-on-the-talk show story has been around for years; in fact, it's so entrenched in the culture that previous versions had the predictor appearing on shows hosted by Phil Donahue and Johnny Carson, both of whom retired long ago.

UL FOOTNOTE. On Nov. 1, 1991, just one day after Halloween, a student at the University of Iowa went berserk and shot up the campus, killing four and injuring two before he turned the gun on himself. Weirdly, though, the University of Iowa was one campus where there had never been widespread repetition of the Halloween Killer rumor.

The daughter's letter home

O h, the combination of pride and heartbreak when your daughter goes away to college, a thousand miles from the loving comfort and warm embrace of home life. Remember how it was all tears and hugs when you said goodbye to her in late August? But now it's late October and you haven't talked to her on the phone for several weeks. She promised to write every day, but all you've received are a few quick notes and the occasional e-mail with hardly any details of her life on campus. Can it be that your little girl has changed so much, that she doesn't really need you any more?

Then—what do you find when you log on to the family computer? A message from your dear daughter, and a long one at that! You knew she'd come through. Finally, you get some detailed information about her life as a college freshman. You call out to your wife, who excitedly joins you at the computer as you click on the message and begin to read:

Dear Mom and Dad:

Well, it's been nearly three months since I said goodbye to you and began my collegiate career. Please accept my apologies for not talking to you more on the phone or sending you longer notes. You've been in my thoughts every day, but things have been so hectic here.

Okay, here goes. I hope you're sitting down, and I hope that as you read this, you remember how much I love you. You're not going to like what you'll learn, so brace yourselves.

Oh God, where do I start? How about some good news? You can hardly notice the scar on my forehead, which is pretty remarkable considering I received 47 stitches after I cracked my head open jumping out of my dorm window when the building caught fire. I spent only a few days in the hospital, and my vision is almost totally restored now, so I feel very lucky. It sure could have been worse!

One of the heroes to emerge from the night of the fire was a local, a gas station attendant, who works near campus and happened to be in the area at the time. He was the one who saw me jump from my dorm window, and he called the fire department and the paramedics. He also visited me every day in the hospital, and when it turned out the dorm was going to have to be closed for extensive repairs, he was kind enough to offer me a place to stay—in the basement of his parents' home. I must tell you, they're wonderful people when they're not drinking. They've already accepted me as their daughter-in-law, even though a wedding date hasn't been set yet. I know this is sudden, but don't worry—you guys will be invited to the wedding, too! Dad, I can't imagine getting married to Bruno without you walking me down the aisle with me wearing Mom's dress—that is, if I can still fit into it and the pregnancy doesn't begin to show.

That's right, I'm with child. I know you guys have always looked forward to the day when you'd become grandparents; well, that day is about seven months away! Congratulations.

I know you will welcome Bruno into the family with open arms. He is a kind and thoughtful person—and though he's not well educated, he's quite ambitious. Even though he's of a different race and religion than ours, I know that your oft-expressed views on tolerance and understanding will carry you through the initial difficulty of accepting a black man into the family. He's a strong and brave man, and I really don't blame him for passing on his infection to me, as he wasn't even aware he had syphilis until we got the blood tests for our impending nuptials. I'm sure you'll welcome him to the table when we come home for fall break. That is, if we can make it home. I had to cash in the ticket you sent me to lend Bruno some money to pay off the interest on his gambling debts. If we can't scrounge up enough money for plane tickets (Bruno says he's got "something big" in the works, so keep your fingers crossed), we can always hitchhike.

Now that I have brought you up to date, I'd like to tell you this, Mom and Dad:

There was no dorm fire. I did not crack open my head. I was not in the hospital. I don't know any gas station attendant named Bruno, I'm not pregnant, I don't have syphilis, and I'm still in possession of the plane ticket you sent me.

However, I am getting a D in sociology and an F in algebra. I just told you the rest of that stuff so you'd be able to put this news in perspective.

⊠ ⊠ ⊠

This story surfaced in the mid-1960s, not as an e-mail message of course, but as a daughter's letter home from college. You can see it as a kind of commentary on the times, with the supposedly liberal parents shocked that their daughter is getting involved in all sorts of mishaps, with the twist being that the supposed wild child really isn't tuning in or turning on or dropping out, she's just having trouble with a couple of freshman courses. What a relief! Sure puts things in perspective, doesn't it?

If a kid ever did write a letter like that, you'd want to smack her, but you'd also have to admit she was a sharp one who should probably change her major to creative writing.

Secrets of fraternity and sorority rituals

I've heard and read about all sorts of bizarre and secret "Greek" rituals—many of them involving the consumption of much alcohol and the slaughtering of a chicken or goat—but it's impossible to get any frat brothers or sorority sisters to divulge the secrets of their snobby little cults.

When I asked a friend who had been in a fraternity about the mystery surrounding these secret rituals, he said, "If you're so interested in learning about these things, why don't you contact the Library of Congress? They've been collecting this stuff for years. It's all on the record."

According to popular lore, the Library of Congress started cataloging these rituals in the 1950s, when Sen. Joseph McCarthy's House Committee on Un-American Activities demanded that all fraternities and sororities turn over their secrets to the government, just to prove they weren't communist sympathizers. The information was collected in a volume that still sits in the Library of Congress, where anyone can peruse it for the asking. In fact, the deepest secrets of every fraternity and sorority in the country—with one exception—are contained in the volume. That one exception is the fraternity of Lambda Chi

Alpha, of which then-President Harry Truman was a member. Truman gave his personal assurance that there was nothing subversive about Lambda Chi, and thus there was no reason for its secrets to be divulged.

Lambda Chi is the only fraternity to be given such an exemption.

Other than Kappa Alpha, that is. FBI director J. Edgar Hoover was a KA, and he saw to it that his fraternity's secrets were not spilled, either.

...And Tau Kappa Epsilon, popularly known as the "Tekes." They eventually were given an exemption, because Ronald Reagan was a brother with Tau Kappa Epsilon, and when he was elected president one of his first official acts was to get TKE's secrets removed from the books.

Also catching a break was Sigma Chi, of which Barry Goldwater was a member. Goldwater lobbied his old colleague and onetime presidential foe Lyndon Johnson to have Sigma Chi's rituals erased from the Library of Congress' collection, and LBJ was happy to oblige.

In the 1990s, powerful women began to exert their influence to get favored sororities removed from the volume. Geraldine Ferraro, Dianne Feinstein, Hillary Clinton and Elizabeth Dole took care of their own sororities.

That's an awful lot of exemptions, isn't it? I wonder how many fraternities and sororities still have their secrets exposed in the LOC record book.

Actually, that number would top out at zero. Not because influential alumni have protected their Greek brothers and sisters, but because no such collection was ever put together in the first place. If you call the LOC and start asking questions about this, it won't be long before you're cut off by some poor soul who has already had to address this issue a thousand times. In fact, this myth is so widespread that the Library of Congress uses a form letter to refute it. An excerpt:

"The Library of Congress receives frequent inquiries concerning college fraternity and sorority publications, particularly those detailing secret initiation rites. The Library's general collections do not include any publications which detail secret initiation rites for specific fraternities. The rumor that a collection of documents detailing specific initiation rites exists at the Library of Congress stems from the belief that such publications were requested either by the House Committee on Un-American Activities or by Sen. Joseph McCarthy's Subcommittee of the Senate Government Operations Committee in the 1950s. We have been unable to identify any information to support this...Unpublished materials from these committees are in the custody of the National Archives and Records Administration and are still sealed. No checklist or indexes exist for these documents."

So all you Greeks out there can rest easy. Your secrets are safe.

The campus scream session

This happened about 20 years ago at Brown University.

Wait—maybe it was UCLA.

No, I believe it was Florida State.

In any case, I wouldn't be surprised if this one turns up as a scene in *Scream 3*, or *Urban Legend 2*, or some other youth-oriented horror movie.

Here's how it was told to me by a friend who attended an Ivy League school:

"For years, dating back to the 1930s, there was a tradition on campus during Finals Week. There's a lot of pressure on everyone at crunch time, so about halfway through the grind of exams, there would be a designated time when everyone on campus was supposed to stop whatever they were doing and scream as loud as possible for five straight minutes.

I've heard it started with just a couple of guys yelling their lungs out, and by the 1960s it had developed into this tradition that was even recognized by the administration as a healthy and harmless way to blow off steam. It was up to the senior class president to designate the date and time of the 'scream session,' and then it was posted all over campus, even listed in the school newspaper. Sometimes the scream session would take place in the middle of the day, sometimes it was held at midnight. There was no set time for it.

"So one year, I think it was back in the 1970s, the scream session was to be held at 10 p.m. on a Thursday. The announcement was made early in the week so there was plenty of time to spread the word on campus.

"Apparently there was this guy who lived off-campus, a strange guy who had been kicked out of school a few years earlier. He went on a couple of dates with a beautiful freshman girl, but she quickly realized the guy was a major creep and told him not to call her any more. But he was obsessed with her, and he kept calling her and showing up at her dormitory and sending her weird letters. It got to the point where she contacted the local police, but they told her there was really nothing they could do beyond telling the guy to back off. The creep promised the police he wouldn't bother her any more, and actually kept to his promise—until the week of finals, that is.

"It was Thursday night about 10 o'clock, and the girl was leaving the library by herself when she was grabbed by the guy and dragged into a stairwell. She started to cry for help, but just then the clock struck 10, and thousands of students all over campus began the five-minute scream session.

For five long agonizing minutes, the poor girl's cries were completely lost, as the deranged creep molested her and then stabbed her repeatedly with a butcher knife. By 10:05, when the screaming faded, she was dead, and her killer had already fled the scene. To this day he's never been found.

"After the body was found, police couldn't figure out why no one on campus had heard the poor girl's cries for help. But then someone put two and two together and said, 'I think we can establish the exact time of this girl's death. It was at 10 p.m., when the screaming started all over campus.'

"That was the end of the scream session at my school—although there are some students who claim you can hear the eerie echoes of a young woman's screams every Thursday during Finals Week, at just about 10 p.m."

Can't you just picture some perky actress from *Dawson's Creek* or *Felicity* getting the part of the unfortunate freshman in the movie version of this UL?

The story of the "scream session attack" has been told and retold on dozens of campuses for at least 20 years, with little variation in the details. Not surprisingly, I was unable to find any concrete proof that it ever took place on any campus.

Exam scams

At Urban Legend University, there's a constant battle going on between lazy but clever students who are trying to scam their way through exams by any means necessary, and savvy world-wise professors who attempt to thwart these students with some creative solutions of their own. Each of the following stories is so delicious you'll wish they were true—and, as always, it's impossible to make the claim that none of these incidents ever took place.

There's certainly no shortage of students and alumni who will swear one or more of these episodes have occurred at their school, whether that school is Ohio State, Yale, North Carolina, USC, Texas A&M, Grambling, Brown, Case Western or Slippery Rock. Amazing how such incredible tales are seemingly cloned through the years.

The stolen exam

There's a scene in *Animal House* where the underachieving Delta boys purloin the carbon of a final exam from a garbage can. Only problem is, the dreaded Omegas are onto the game, and they've switched the real final for a phony version, leaving the Deltas hopelessly unprepared for the big test.

That was the one and only moral lesson in *Animal House*, thank God.

In the urban legend of the stolen exam, it's the teacher who puts a roadblock in the thieving student's attempt to cheat his way to glory. On the day before the test, the student meets with professor, who tells him he needs to get an 'A' on the final or he'll fail the course. The student starts to make his case for leniency, but the professor is called away from the office for a moment. Filled with anxiety, the student paces around the room and pokes around—and that's when he comes across a stack of tests. The final exams, just sitting out in the open! He quickly snatches one copy and jams it into his coat, just before the professor returns to the office.

"Now where were we?" says the professor.

"I was just leaving," the student replies. "Gotta study for the big test!"

His instructor is confused. Why did the kid's mood change so quickly? If he thinks one night of studying hard is going to adequately prepare him for an exam, let him dream.

The next morning, the instructor counts the tests and realizes one is missing. He had at least a dozen students visit him the day before, and there's no way of knowing which one had the gall to steal a copy of the test—or is there?

Chuckling to himself, the professor takes out a pair of scissors and carefully slices a half-inch from the bottom of each remaining copy of the test. When the students turn in their papers at the end of test, only one literally sticks out—the stolen exam.

Even though the student scored a 96 on the test, he was flunked by the professor, and he didn't utter a peep of protest about it.

The open-book exam

The instructor of a particularly difficult class in Freshman English tells her students she's going to cut them a big break for the final: it's going to be "open-book." As a matter of fact, she says, students may use "anything you can carry into the classroom" to help them with the test.

Nearly everybody in the class takes this to mean they can come in with books, reference guides, handwritten notes, etc. But one smart-ass freshman football player takes the professor's words literally. After all, she's the one who always says you must choose your words carefully—and she did say "anything you can carry," didn't she? So on the day of the exam, he shows up carrying a nerdy little graduate student under his arm.

"And just what do you think you're doing?" says the professor over the titters of the class.

"You said we could use anything we could carry into the classroom," replies the student. "I'm carrying Dilbert, and he'll be taking the test for me."

Trapped by her own words, the professor has no choice but to allow the graduate student to take the exam for the football player, who winds up with an 'A' for the course.

The stack of blue book exams

This happened in one of those big, impersonal classes you have to take your freshman year, with about

300 other people all packed into some gigantic lecture hall where the teacher has to use a microphone and an overhead projector just to communicate with everyone.

For the final exam, the teacher handed out blue books to the students and told them they had exactly two hours to answer as many of the 200 multiple choice questions as possible. He set a timer to go off in 120 minutes and said that when the buzzer went off, everyone had to stop writing immediately, with no exceptions. Violate this rule and you'd receive an automatic 'F.'

Two hours later, the alarm sounded, and the professor commanded everyone to drop their pencils and drop off their blue books on the way out. Everyone began filing out—except one frantic kid who kept scribbling away, desperately trying to pencil in a few more answers even though time had expired.

"You there!" the teacher called out. "If you don't stop writing immediately, you're going to be flunked!"

"I just need a minute more, just one minute!" the student pleaded as he continued to write in the blue book.

At that point, it really didn't matter what he said; by this time, the teacher had already doomed the kid to an automatic 'F.' Most of the class had already turned in their exams by the time the troublemaker finally gathered his things and clomped down the stairs.

"You might as well keep that exam as a souvenir, because you've already failed this course," said the instructor.

"You've got to be kidding me!" the student cried. "I was only one minute late. What difference does it make?"

The teacher was unmoved. "Rules are rules. If I let you have an extra minute I'd have to let everyone have an extra minute, wouldn't I?"

"Do you know who I am?" said the student. "Do you know what my *name* is?"

"No I don't, and I couldn't care less," replied the teacher.

"Good!" said the student—and with that he jammed his blue book right in the middle of the stack before dashing out of there.

🗙 🗙 🗙

I've included this story because I've heard it at least 20 times over the last decade, but to me, there's a gaping flaw in the telling. Okay, the teacher doesn't know the names of all the students in the overcrowded class, so he wouldn't be able to identify the student by name as he's grading the tests. But once he was finished with the grading process, couldn't he require all students to show up, with student IDs, to claim their exams? All he'd have to do is make a face identification of the culprit, hang on to that particular exam and change the grade to an 'F.'

Most urban legends, even the ones that defy logic, have a nice little airtight quality about them; that's why they survive through myriad retellings. This one should fade—not because it's implausible, but because of the obvious way in which the teacher could have nailed the student, thus negating the twist.

The letter home to mom

Once again, the ubiquitous blue book plays a part in an exam scam classic:

Our unprepared student freaks out when he's confronted with a complicated essay question that will count for 100 percent of the test. He has no idea what to say—this is the one portion of the textbook he didn't study! To make matters worse, the professor has given each student *two* blue books, indicating that he expects a long and detailed answer.

And then a light bulb goes off. The student starts writing in a blue book—but he's not answering the question, he's writing a letter to his mother. "I really think I did well on the essay," he writes. "I finished ahead of everyone else in the class so I figured I'd write to you, dear mother. I don't want to get up and leave early—it'll seem like I'm showing off. Anyway, let me tell you about this class. I'm so lucky to have had this teacher! He's by far the smartest and most inspirational teacher I've ever had..."

At the end of the class, the student turns in the letter to mom and then runs back to his dorm room, where he opens the textbook for the class and uses it as a reference guide as he composes a thoughtful and comprehensive answer to the essay question. He then mails that blue book to his mother in Boston.

That night the professor rings the student and says, "I don't know how to tell you this, but we have a big problem."

"You're kidding me," says the student. "To be honest with you, I thought I aced the test."

"You very well might have, for all I know," says the teacher. "I haven't seen your answers."

"I don't understand."

"I've got a letter to your mother here instead of your essay. Does that make any sense to you?"

"Oh no!" says the student, trying his best to sound shocked. "That means I must have mailed the test to my mom. This is the most embarrassing thing that's ever happened to me." The student says he'll call his mother right away and instruct her to send the envelope straight to the professor; that way, the teacher will know the story is legitimate.

Sure enough, an envelope arrives at the professor's office a few days later, and he opens it to find the student's test, which of course contains a beautifully written essay. Not only does the professor give the kid an "A," he sends the other booklet to the student's mother with a note attached telling her what a pleasure it was having the lad in his class.

The flat tire excuse

Three smart (and incredibly cocky) fraternity brothers were so confident they'd ace their chemistry final that they went on a weekend road trip before the exam, which was scheduled for Monday at 10 a.m. They spent all weekend partying with some girls from a nearby school and never once even bothered to pick up a book, even though the final was going to count for 50 percent of their grade.

Problem was, they overslept Monday morning. By the time they made it back to campus it was noon, and they knew the professor would be busy collecting exam booklets from the other students. Suddenly the "A's" or "B's" they counted on receiving for the class were looking like "D's" at best! Depression set in. What to do?

"I've got the plan!" said one of the brothers as they crossed the quad and headed for the classroom. "We'll tell the professor we were doing a charity thing—like a dance marathon—and we overslept this morning because we were so tired from dancing, and as we were racing back to campus, we got a flat tire and it took forever to get the thing fixed."

The three charmers told the story to their stupid professor, who fell for it hook, line, and sinker.

"All right boys, I'm not going to penalize you for your good intentions, even though you should have given yourselves more time to return to campus," he said. "I'll see you here bright and early tomorrow morning. You'll have two hours to take the exam." The frat boys exchanged knowing glances on the way out the door. Any teacher who falls for that deserves to get taken for a ride. The boys spent the rest of the day studying to reassure themselves, and their cocky swagger had returned by the next morning, when they entered the empty classroom.

"There's nobody in either of the adjoining classrooms, so each of you gets your own room," said the professor. "Not that I'd accuse you boys of cheating or anything, but we'll play it on the safe side."

These guys didn't care, as they weren't *cheaters* or anything; they were just resourceful types who had figured out a way to buy a little time from their unsophisticated instructor.

In the separate classrooms, each young man tackled the exam. The first question was worth 5 points, and was a breeze. At about the same time, each of the boys flipped to the second page, where they found the following message:

"Question #2 (worth 95 points): Which tire went flat?"

The cries of anguish could be heard through the building. Of course, the boys never discussed which tire supposedly went flat.

Chapter Three
Legends of the Silver Screen

In the summer of 1998, I interviewed Mickey Rooney, who told me a story about his days as a child prodigy. "When I was five years old," he said. "I went to Walt Disney's office for lunch. He was drawing at his desk, and I climbed onto his lap and said, 'Whatcha drawing, Uncle Walt?'"

"He showed me this drawing of a mouse and told me it was for a new cartoon he was working on. He said he was thinking of calling him Marty Mouse, and what did I think of that name?"

"I told him I had a better name—mine. I said, 'Why don't you call him Mickey Mouse, Uncle Walt?'"

Disney said, 'I just might do that.'

You gotta love Mickey Rooney. For one thing, he was born in 1920, which means he was eight, not five, when Mickey Mouse debuted in the cartoon *Steamboat Willie*. For another, Walt Disney came up with the idea and the name for the mouse while he was taking a train home after learning his first cartoon series, *Alice Comedies*, had been canceled.

And there is no record of little Mickey Rooney being on that train.

But it's a harmless tale, and besides, we all know that Hollywood is a make-believe place populated by make-believe people who tell make-believe stories about their make-believe lives. The quotes attributed to stars and studio heads, the tidy anecdotes told through the years about casting decisions and movie-star romances and the creation of classic films—a lot of these juicy tales are spiced heavily with apocryphal details.

Do stories like the one told by Mickey Rooney qualify as urban legends? Well, maybe they're glamorous cousins to the UL...

The ghost in *Three Men and a Baby*

A year or so after the release of the comedy *Three Men and a Baby* on video, a *Sun-Times* reader called to tell me there was something really scary about that movie.

"There's a ghost of a dead little boy in the background of one scene."

"Of course there is," I said, before gently suggesting the caller double the dosage of whatever medication he was taking.

Little did I know the reader was right—sort of.

When *Three Men and a Baby* was released in 1987, nary a word was said about any eerie ghost-boy. But after it was out on video for a while, stories began circulating about a ghostly figure who had made an unscheduled and inexplicable cameo in the otherwise harmless comedy.

The apparition appears in a scene in which Jack Holden (Ted Danson) is visited by his mother (Celeste Holm) in the trendy loft apartment Jack shares with his two bachelor buddies. As Jack's mom cradles the infant in her arms, the chilling image of a little boy appears behind curtains in a background window, but neither character makes mention of it. Why should they? It's obviously not a part of the story itself.

Nobody on the set saw the boy while the scene was being filmed, but he's clearly visible to anyone who rents the movie. Only later did the filmmakers learn that a 9-year-old boy committed suicide with a shotgun in the very apartment they had selected as the home for the three men and their baby, and the figure in the background is the ghost of that poor little boy. If you watch closely, you can see the curtains move, revealing a shotgun in the ghost's grip.

The boy's parents had moved out of the trendy apartment after the terrible tragedy but had been unable to sell the place, which explains why such a great locale was available to the movie company at a bargain rate.

When the boy's mother saw *Three Men and a Baby* for the first time on video, she let out a blood-curdling scream as she recognized the image of her son—in his funeral clothes, no less. She tried to get the producers to cut the scene or edit it in some way, but they refused. So she made the talk show rounds, telling Phil Donahue and Oprah Winfrey and Geraldo Rivera of her anguish and suffering. Unfortunately, even the publicity blitz couldn't ease her pain, and she ended up in a mental institution, where she remains to this day.

Or so the story goes. In reality, the "ghost" is a cardboard cutout of Ted Danson in top hat and tails. (It's not life-size, which is why people thought the "ghost" was a little boy.) His character in the movie, you might recall, was an actor, and the original script called for a running joke about a dog food commercial in which Danson's character appeared in formal wear. That element didn't make it into the final version of the movie, but the cardboard cutout makes a couple of appearances—first near the window, and then later in the movie, when the baby's mother (Nancy Travis) returns to reclaim the baby.

And for the record: the supposedly haunted apartment was created on a soundstage. It is not real.

The munchkin suicide

You probably never thought about this, but munchkins are people, too, and they can fall in love just like everyone else. That means they can get their little munchkin hearts broken to the point where they don't want to go on living their little munchkin lives any more.

Such was the case with the munchkin actor who was so devastated about being dumped by a female little person that he committed suicide, hanging himself on the set of *The Wizard of Oz*—a death that was inadvertently captured during filming and somehow made its way into the final print of the movie.

I rented a copy of *The Wizard of Oz* and skipped forward to the legendary scene where you can supposedly view the munchkin swaying from a tree. We pick up the action as Dorothy (Judy Garland) and the Scarecrow (Ray Bolger) are following the Yellow Brick Road on their way to the Emerald City. They meet the Tin Man (Jack Haley), and are confronted by the Wicked Witch of the West (Margaret Hamilton), who tries to torch the unfortunate Scarecrow.

Stay with the scene to the end, as Dorothy, the Tin Man, and the Scarecrow proceed to make their way down the Yellow Brick Road and away from the camera. There in the trees is some sort of movement—perhaps the eerie form of a sad munchkin, hanging himself.

Other rumors said it wasn't a suicide, it was just a hapless stagehand who had taken a tumble from the rafters. In either case, there's no doubt something is occurring in those trees. Nobody noticed it when the movie was released in 1939 or during any of the subsequent theatrical reissues over the years—but when a special-edition, 50th anniversary video was issued in 1989, *Oz* buffs noticed the rustling in the trees, and an urban legend was born. (That Judy Garland would often appear on talk shows in the 1950s and 1960s, telling greatly exaggerated tales of munchkin shenanigans probably added some credibility to the notion of a munchkin suicide caught on film.)

So what exactly are we seeing in that scene? According to a number of *Oz* experts, including the narrator on *The Ultimate Oz* laser disc, it's a bird. The scene in question was shot on a soundstage. In order to make the set look more "real," the filmmakers used a number of exotic birds, including peacocks, emus, and cranes. As Dorothy, the Tin Man, and the Scarecrow head away from the camera, a large bird rustles in the trees and spreads its wings.

Stephen Cox, author of *The Munchkins of Oz* (1996), advanced this explanation in a 1997 column by Cecil "The Straight Dope" Adams. Cox told Adams he'd heard the suicide theory, but what we're seeing is a large bird—"maybe a crane or stork," writes Adams. Whatever make and model of bird we're looking at, it's nothing more than a slight distraction, and since director Victor Fleming wanted birds in the scene in the first place, there was no reason to shoot another take.

In a 1996 interview with the *Orlando Sentinel*, then-81-year-old Meinhardt Raabe, who played the coroner of Munchkin Land (the man who had the qualifications to say if a witch was "not only merely dead, but really most sincerely dead") said he'd never heard the hanging munchkin rumor until about 1993, but of course it wasn't true: "They put an Australian emu in the background...it's crazy, like watching clouds in the sky. People see all sorts of things in Oz."

Back to the Future II predicts World Series

The original *Back to the Future*, with Michael J. Fox as time-traveling high school student Marty McFly, was a clever and entertaining romp that deserved its critical and commercial kudos. Fox and the rest of the cast were uniformly excellent, the script and direction were sharp and lively, and the tunes from Huey Lewis and the News were perfect for the mood of the film. They should have left well enough alone, but of course they didn't. Alas, *Back to the Future II* and the imaginatively titled *Back to the Future III* were jumbled, garish, convoluted and just plain stupid.

There is, however, one redeeming element to *BTTF II*, and that is the contribution of a pretty decent urban legend to the popular culture. According to movie buff lore, the 1989 movie correctly forecasts the 1997 Word Series triumph of the Florida Marlins—a prediction made even more astounding when you consider that the Marlins didn't even exist in 1989!

However, it's only about 10 percent true. The movie picks up where *Back to the Future* ends, with Christopher Lloyd's Doc Brown telling Marty there's a problem with his kids. Wandering around in the year 2015, Marty sees a holographic sports broadcast announcing that the Chicago Cubs have won the World Series by defeating "Miami." (No nickname is given for the team.) He's distracted by this announcement as an old man approaches and asks him for a donation to save the clock tower.

The joke is that the woeful Cubs finally win the World Series, and the mention of Miami being in the Series was a nod to the inevitable expansion that would have taken place by 2015. There was no Miami team in the major leagues in the late 1980s, but it would be a pretty safe bet that such a large metropolis would have its own club by then.

There was no reason for this episode to spawn an urban legend when the movie came out, but when the Florida Marlins shocked the world by upsetting the Cleveland Indians in the 1997 World Series, some movie fans with inaccurate memories of *BTTF II* started talking about how the movie actually foresaw the Marlins' miracle season. Some versions of the rumor had either Marty or his rival Biff saying something like, "That'll be the day" when they hear the announcement of the World Series victory.

None of this happens in the film. It's the Cubs, not the unnamed Miami team, who are named as the World Series champs—and besides, the broadcast in the movie has to do with the 2015 season. Why would a program on the air in 2015 be announcing the results of the 1997 Series?

The Marisa Tomei Oscar mistake

It's hard to make the case that Marisa Tomei's performance as the long-suffering girlfriend of Joe Pesci in the 1992 comedy *My Cousin Vinny* was worthy of an Academy Award. She was adorable, all right, and she had the Brooklyn accent down cold, but come on. If Marisa's work was Oscar-worthy, why did the Academy snub Ralph Macchio from the same movie for Best Supporting Actor?

Even after Tomei was nominated, she was considered a longshot. The Supporting Actress field was loaded that year with esteemed actors in prestige projects: Miranda Richardson in *Damage*, Joan Plowright in *Enchanted April*, Vanessa Redgrave in *Howard's End*, and Judy Davis in *Husbands and Wives*. Take a look at that list and you can see few people were picking Marisa Tomei from *My Cousin Vinny*.

Traditionally at the Academy Awards, the previous year's winner in a similar category announces the nominees and the winner, so for the 1993 ceremony, the presenter for Best Supporting Actress was Jack Palance, who had won the Best Supporting Actor trophy the previous year for *City Slickers*. Palance stumbled a bit as he read the names of the nominees; then he tore open the envelope and said, "And the Oscar goes to...Marisa Tomei for *My Cousin Vinny*."

A ripple of surprise ran through the audience, with Tomei looking more surprised than anyone. She was probably thinking to herself, *There must be some kind of mistake*.

She wouldn't be the only one entertaining such a thought. The curtain had barely dropped on the 1993 Academy Awards ceremony when the rumors began circulating about Tomei's shocking victory. According to the story, the elderly Palance—who did seem a bit shaky and lost during his appearance—had a made a horrible mistake when it was time to read the winner. Instead of calling out Vanessa Redgrave's name, he became confused and read Tomei's name because alphabetically she was the last of the five nominees, and her name was still on the TelePrompter. Before he could correct his error, the music had swelled up, Tomei had popped out of her seat and the audience members had recovered from their surprise and were giving the startled young actress a hearty round of applause.

The confused Palance never had a chance to say another word, and officials from the Academy decided to cover up the whole thing, rather than risk their credibility by admitting the gaffe. Some say Tomei was informed backstage of the mix-up but refused to part with her trophy; others claim she's still in the dark, although she's no doubt heard the rumors by now.

This rumor became so widespread by 1994 that the *Hollywood Reporter* did a story about the supposed foulup, making the claim that it was being circulated by the "former son-in-law of a distinguished Academy Award winner." Huh? Why would the *former* son-in-law of some old Oscar winner want to spread such a tale? What would be the upside for him? And anyway, how would he know?

A few years later, a famous film critic made a few television appearances in which he claimed the Tomei story was true, and that there was a massive cover-up in Hollywood to keep the public in the dark. Of course, he offered no proof of any such conspiracy.

The Orange County, California *Register* attempted to kill the story in a 1994 article, "For Outstanding Achievement in the Art of Oscar Rumors," and my colleague at the *Sun-Times*, Roger Ebert, also tried to douse it in a 1997 feature. Nevertheless, there are those who believe to this day that Marisa Tomei should scratch her name off that Academy Award and hand it over to Ms. Redgrave.

Here's the official explanation from the Motion Picture Academy. At every Academy Awards ceremony since 1953, two accountants from the firm of Price Waterhouse are stationed in the wings for the duration of the ceremony. These individuals know the names of all the winners well beforehand; in fact, they are the only two people who have this knowledge in advance. They have standing instructions to immediately go onstage and make a correction if the wrong name is read for any reason.

To date, that has never happened. Marisa Tomei won the 1992 Academy Award fair and square, and no amount of petty squabbling, irresponsible rumor-mongering, or jealous backbiting can take that away from her.

The Twister tornado

Boy those people in *Twister* were idiots. Every time they got wind (so to speak) of a big tornado, they'd pack up their whiz-bang scientific equipment, hop into their pickup trucks and chase right after the storm, all the while whooping it up and cranking the stereo as if they were on the way to Spring Break or something.

These weren't ordinary tornadoes, either; these were monster tornadoes that could fling cows around, tornadoes that actually made ominous groaning noises that sounded like the shark's soundtrack in *Jaws*. How does a wispy Helen Hunt stand a chance against something like that?

Even though the so-called plot of *Twister* was about as complicated as a *game* of Twister, I have to admit the movie was wildly entertaining, due mostly to the incredible special effects that made you feel as if the characters were facing off against real tornadoes and not blank screens and computer-generated effects.

If you saw the movie in a theater with a top quality screen and sound system, you were practically pinned in your seat—and if you happened to catch *Twister* on a certain night at a particular drive-in located in southern

Ontario, Canada, you really thought the special effects were amazing, especially when the tornado appeared to blast right through the screen.

In an incredible twist(er) of fate, the movie was playing at a drive-in theater just outside Thorgold, Ontario, when a real tornado tore through the area, causing extensive property damage. Incredibly, the tornado's path cut right through the drive-in screen during one of the tornado sequences in the movie, creating the most realistic 3-D effect in the history of cinema. No one at the theater was injured by the blast, but the screen was destroyed. Patrons were offered refunds, but many of them said they didn't want their money back, as they'd never been so entertained in their lives.

🗙 🗙 🗙

The *London Daily Telegraph* was among the newspapers reporting this story. In a May 24, 1996 column, Mark Steyn wrote about one of the patrons who was at the drive-in theater when the tornado supposedly struck: "During one of the duller scenes, one guy went to the bathroom, and came back to find the screen vibrating wildly and a loud whooshing filling the air. Pleasantly surprised to find that for once the effects and Surround sound were all they were cracked up to be, he took a moment to realize it was a real twister. Seconds later, the screen was ripped out of the ground and came crashing down on top of the cars, sending the crowd fleeing for their lives. I'd like to think God was reminding the audience that He is the ultimate special effect..."

That must have been one incredibly stupid man, to think even for a split second that he was witnessing spectacular special effects and not *standing in the middle of a tornado!*

Let's set the urban legend aside and review the facts. It is true that on May 20, 1996, a tornado struck the town of Thorgold—and the screen at a drive-in theater called the Can-View 4 did sustain damage. And sure enough, the movie *Twister* was scheduled to play on that particular screen.

However, the tornado struck during the light of day, and we all know drive-in movies don't open until after dark.

A
Titanic
timeframe

It's hard to believe now, but before *Titanic* became a
billion-dollar triumph at the box office and a huge success at the Academy Awards, there were grave doubts
about the commercial viability of the movie. Not wanting
to take a financial bath all by itself, Paramount ended up
sharing the frighteningly high production costs with Twen-
tieth Century Fox, and James Cameron even forfeited his
director's fee so a few million more could be poured into
the budget. In the fall of 1997, with *Titanic* set to launch
in December of that year, advance buzz on the movie
was mixed at best.

So there was much concern when Cameron's first cut
came in with a running time of nearly four hours. Even
with some last-minute trims, *Titanic* had a daunting length
of three hours, 14 minutes. Not only would this limit the
number of times the film could be shown in a day, but
there was great concern that audiences wouldn't want to
sit in a theater that long, regardless of how strong the
reviews might be.

In a *Los Angeles Times* story published in December of 1997, about three weeks before the film was to be
released, an executive on the film was asked about the

last-minute cuts Cameron had made. "The movie went from three hours, 36 minutes, to two hours, 74 minutes," said the exec.

From that joking response, an urban myth was launched. Soon the gossip world was buzzing with stories that theater owners—who are usually leery of any movies that run for more than three hours—had been duped into thinking *Titanic* wasn't three hours long because it was being promoted as having on official time of "two hours, 74 minutes."

Check out this *Good Morning America* transcript from Dec. 31, 1997, as reviewer Joel Siegel jokingly discusses the issue with anchor Tom Bergeron:

SIEGEL: Three hours go by in a minute, and it's doing incredible business. This Friday, it'll hit $100 million, considering they only get one show a night.

BERGERON: That's right.

SIEGEL: Now, it's bad luck to have a three-hour movie, so they're advertising it as two hours and 74 minutes long.

Two weeks later, on Jan. 15, 1998, Siegel revisited the topic with Charles Gibson and Nancy Snyderman.

SIEGEL: [*Titanic* has] grossed over $200 million. It's amazing, because it's the first movie ever, I think, to gross more than $20 million four weekends in a row.

GIBSON: Wow.

SNYDERMAN: Oh, that's interesting, a new stat.

SIEGEL: A new stat. And it's long. They only get one showing a night.

SNYDERMAN: Yes.

SIEGEL: Because the movie—

SNYDERMAN: It's three hours plus.

SIEGEL: Three hours and 14 minutes. Although it's supposed to be the kiss of death in Hollywood, they have a movie over three hours, so they're advertising it as two hours and 74 minutes long—which is actually longer than it took the ship to sink. It took the ship two hours and 40 minutes to sink; it takes you two hours and 74 minutes to see the movie.

Siegel was obviously having fun with the story, but his comments only served to fuel the silly fire.

It's a bit of a misconception that it's bad luck for a movie to run more than three hours. Obviously that didn't hold true for *Titanic,* nor did three-hour-plus running times hurt *Schindler's List, Dances With Wolves* or *Braveheart,* all huge commercial successes and Academy Award winners for Best Picture. As for theater owners, they probably would prefer movies to run less than two hours—that way you get more customers in your lobby to buy popcorn—but you still have more than one showing per night if a film runs three hours. Theaters were showing *Titanic* at 3:30 p.m., 7 p.m., and 10:30 p.m., for example. And in this age of multi-screen megaplexes, viewers had the opportunity to see the movie practically every hour.

Nevertheless, the story that Paramount was "advertising" the running length at two hours and 74 minutes continued to grow. There was even a bogus posting on the Internet of a London newspaper story saying that some Brits were offended by the American studio's attempt to fool them into thinking the movie wasn't all that long.

Well, the article doesn't exist—because the studio never tried to pull such a stunt, overseas or anywhere else. Greg Brilliant, vice-president of national publicity for Paramount, said, "Paramount never had another running time for *Titanic*. We never officially promoted it that way. It was an inside running joke in Hollywood, but there was never a statement issued or anything."

Besides, studios almost never list the running time of a movie in their advertising materials; check your local paper's movie section and you'll see what I mean. It's true that many film reviewers include the movie's length in the credit boxes that run with the text, but in those cases the running time is almost always listed in pure minutes. So in the case of *Titanic*, the length was listed at 194 minutes.

UL FOOTNOTE. Does Arnold Schwarzenegger make a cameo appearance in *Titanic*? That was the rumor going around when the movie was released on video. Supposedly Cameron had completely run out of money, but he needed a few shots for the ballroom sequence, so he spliced in a few quick cuts from the opening of *True Lies*, in which secret agent Arnold spins around the dance floor of a black-tie ball with Tia Carrera.

Doubtful. For one thing, the costumes wouldn't have matched, what with *Titanic* taking place more than 80 years ago, and *True Lies* set in modern times. Besides, Arnold Schwarzenegger is four times the size of Leonardo DiCaprio, and he would have stuck out like a linebacker at a Pee-Wee football game.

Disney secret messages

For years, the Walt Disney Company denied or simply ignored all rumors and reports about subliminal messages or naughty images cropping up in their wildly popular and wholesome full-length feature cartoons.

Until *The Rescuers* controversy. This R-rated moment Disney had to acknowledge, because it wasn't an urban myth, it was undisputedly real.

You had to go about 38 minutes into a tainted copy of *The Rescuers* to catch a glimpse of the little picture that, in January of 1999, prompted Disney to recall more than 3.4 million copies of the 1977 animated feature.

In the offending scene, a couple of mice named Bernard and Bianca are flying through town in a small box strapped to the back of an albatross. When they pass by a particular building, a topless woman can be glimpsed through a window. It's not visible at normal speed, as the image appears on just two of the movie's 110,000-plus frames. You have to hit the pause button on the VCR and do a frame-by-frame advance. Eventually, you see the naked torso of a grownup gal. Then it disappears for a moment before showing up again, in the same window.

It's not exactly a shocking image, even for a Disney cartoon. Heck, the title character in *Pocahantas* looked, moved and talked like Christy Turlington, and Esmerelda's pole-dance in *The Hunchback of Notre Dame* was nearly as provocative as Elizabeth Berkley's gyrations in *Showgirls*—and those were intentional images.

The images in *The Rescuers*, however, left no room for interpretation. You couldn't claim people were really looking at a window plant or a lamp or a pillow—it was a topless woman, no doubt about it. The honchos at Disney had little choice but to recall the movie, which was issued on video in December 1998 after theatrical showings in 1977, 1983 and 1989. (*The Rescuers* was first released on video in 1992, but a Disney spokesman said those copies were made from a different print, which didn't contain the topless woman's cameo.) Supposedly, the handiwork was not the product of some mischievous animator, but someone messing around during post-production.

"This was something that was done more than 20 years ago," said a Disney spokesman, who categorized the controversy as "an internal matter." And a particularly embarrassing and exasperating situation for Disney, what with all those rumors in the past about subliminal images in films.

Let's take a look at some of the more enduring stories, and whether the claims about them have any veracity whatsoever.

In *The Little Mermaid*, there was a widespread report that in the first wedding scene (where a disguised Ursula tries to wed Prince Eric), the minister becomes visibly aroused. After taking another look at this sequence, I'd have to say this one is total bunk. The minister is kneeling; those are his *knees* sticking out from under his tunic.

You'd have to be a sex-obsessed, insanely repressed blue-nose to see anything else. I guess that explains why some ultra-conservative groups bleated long and loud about.

Less clear-cut was the supposedly suggestive message appearing in *The Lion King*. Lore has it that the letters S-E-X appear in a cloud of dust at one point, but again, you see what you want to see. It does seem as if three letters are formed in the sky, but to me it looks more like S-F-X, which is movie-speak for "special effects." Maybe an animator was having a little fun putting in a plug for the technical wizards.

Either that or it's just a cloud of dust.

Then there's the claim that in *Aladdin* the title character blurts, "All good teenagers take off their clothes!"

Here we're getting into grassy knoll territory. At some point you have to ask *why* the incredibly successful Disney empire would risk its status as the Unofficial Sponsor of America's Childhood by inserting stupidly suggestive words or images in movies destined to earn hundreds of millions of dollars in profits. For that matter, why would some Disney employee risk a thriving career with a great company on a silly little practical joke?

Apparently these thoughts didn't occur to *Movie Guide* magazine, a Christian entertainment publication, which in 1995 ran a story about the "take off your clothes" line and drew comparisons to the heavy metal bands of old that supposedly "backmasked" Satanic messages into their albums. According to an article in the *Wall Street Journal* that detailed the controversy, the magazine exhorted "moral Americans" to contact Disney chairman Michael Eisner and ask him to remove his movies' "manipulative subliminal messages." The article prompted conservative groups such as the American Life League to protest, which led to an *Associated Press* article on the controversy, which meant dozens of mainstream newspapers picked up on it. Nobody seemed to notice or care when the publisher of *Movie Guide* finally got around to viewing *Aladdin* and quickly printed a retraction because he realized Disney was telling the truth.

(Freeze-frame alert: According to the book *Mouse Under Glass* by David Koenig, *Aladdin* supposedly also contains more "traditional" hidden treats. For example, in a scene where Jafar enters a room and a stack of toys collapses, one of the toys is the Beast from *Beauty and the Beast*. And, at the end of the movie, when Rajah grows from a cub to a tiger, he sprouts a Mickey Mouse head for a split second.)

$$\boxtimes \ \boxtimes \quad \boxtimes$$

The Rescuers doesn't mark the first time a fleeting surprise has appeared in a Disney film. The theatrical, early videocassette, and laserdisc versions of *Who Framed Roger Rabbit* (which is not a children's movie) reportedly contained a number of racy images, including Baby Huey extending his middle finger, a mini-skirted and panty-less Jessica Rabbit briefly flashing the audience, and graffiti on a men's room wall stating, "For a Good Time Call Allyson Wonderland." In the climactic scene, Winnie the Pooh's sidekick, Piglet, was glimpsed hanging off a caboose—and in every window in that train there's a violent act taking place. However, those alleged pranks do not appear in the video of *Who Framed Roger Rabbit* that I watched in early 1999.

More benign—but definitely there for the spotting— are the quick cameos in *The Hunchback of Notre Dame*. According to Disneyphiles, if you freeze-frame your way through the second musical number, you'll spot Belle from *Beauty and the Beast*, Pumbaa from *The Lion King* and a merchant who has the flying carpet from *Aladdin*. (There's also what appears to be a satellite dish on one roof.)

Given the recent controversy over *The Rescuers*, something tells me the current crop of Disney animators, digitizers and other technical pros will think twice before inserting any unsanctioned tricks into movies. You just wouldn't want to face the wrath of Mickey.

Snuff said

In an early scene from Joel Schumacher's overwrought, yet entertaining 1999 film *8mm*, private investigator Nicolas Cage is summoned to the mansion of a little old lady in a wheelchair whose billionaire businessman husband has just passed away. As the old gal's lawyer explains, the geezer left more than stocks and bonds in his personal safe; there was also a single canister of film, containing searing images of a young girl seemingly being murdered. When the lawyer asks Cage if he knows about the existence of such hideously evil movies, Cage explains that snuff films are "kind of an urban myth."

Except in this movie, of course. *8mm* takes us on a grisly rollercoaster ride as Cage sinks deep into the mire of the underground porn scene, where leather-clad weirdos in cave-like structures hawk sick movies. After following a number of dead-end trails and false leads, Cage discovers snuff films really do exist, courtesy of an infamous filmmaker from New York. We now realize the girl Cage has been hired to find really was murdered on film.

The release of *8mm* sparked renewed debate about whether snuff films exist in the real world. Clarification:

We're not talking about murders, suicides or fatal accidents that have been caught on film or tape, as in the infamous *Faces of Death* shockumentaries (which combine staged scenes with footage of real autopsies and accidents), or the videotape of Pennsylvania public official R. Budd Dwyer shooting himself at a press conference; or *Execution*, a popular video showing the government-mandated deaths of nearly two dozen people in separate incidents.

In a "real" snuff movie, the victim thinks she's appearing in a low-budget thriller or porno movie, but soon realizes the filmmakers aren't going to pretend to kill her, they're going to end her life as the camera rolls. Supposedly there would be a huge market for such a film because it would be showing the real thing.

As of this writing, authorities have never discovered a true snuff film, rumors to the contrary. There are some twisted simulations of snuff movies, e.g., *Flower of Flesh and Blood*, which supposedly so freaked out actor Charlie Sheen that he turned over a copy to the FBI, only to learn it was a fake, and the 1976 piece of junk *Snuff*, which at the time was rumored to contain actual footage of a murder but was in reality just a crummy repackaging of a 1971 movie called *Slaughter*.

There have also been rumors about serial killers such as John Wayne Gacy, "Son of Sam," or Jeffrey Dahmer filming or taping themselves in the act of murder. Charles Manson and his wild-eyed family also were rumored to have made some home movies of their victims. Fortunately, no such movies exist, though there have been cases of killers who have made videotapes of their victims *before* violence was committed, videotapes that of course were valuable pieces of evidence in subsequent trials. About 10 years ago, a couple of clowns from Virginia posted an advertisement on an Internet bulletin board, in which they said they were looking for a young boy to be tortured and killed on camera. When the men were arrested and charged with plotting a kidnapping and murder, they claimed it was all a sick joke, but they ended up serving time for their little prank.

To date, there is no documented evidence of a snuff movie, though in 1998, police in Scotland took possession of several "squish movies," in which women in skimpy garments and high heels were seen stomping frogs, mice and insects to death. I am not kidding.

⊠ ⊠ ⊠

UL FOOTNOTE. *8mm* is not the first mainstream Hollywood film to use a snuff movie as a plot device. In *52 Pick-Up*, a John Frankenheimer film based on an Elmore Leonard novel, businessman Roy Scheider is kidnapped and taken to a remote warehouse, where he is made to watch an amateur movie of his mistress (Kelly Preston) as she is strapped to a chair and gunned down. Adding to Scheider's horror is his realization that he's sitting in the exact same spot shown in the movie, and the blood on the wall behind him is still fresh.

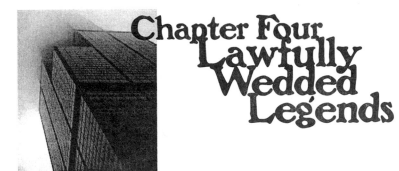

Chapter Four
Lawfully
Wedded
Legends

The wedding experience is fraught with fear, concern, anxiety, trepidation, nervousness, family pressure, financial concerns, the potential for great humiliation—and, oh yes, love. I've never been married, but I've attended dozens of weddings and I've seen hundreds of friends go through the agonizing, tedious, time-consuming and nerve-wracking ordeal that is the prenuptial preparation ritual. The negotiations over who will be invited and who will be snubbed, the efforts to keep the cost of the reception low, the debates about wedding bands and entree selections and bridesmaids' dresses, the fights and the tears and the second thoughts...

No wonder most urban legends about weddings and honeymoons are tales of great humiliation, lasting embarrassment, and/or horrible pain. The prospective brides and grooms who hear these stories can't help but feel better about their own situation...

The philandering groom

This dramatic confrontation has unfolded at hundreds of wedding rehearsal dinners over the last decade, if we're to believe all of the versions of this story in circulation. Sometimes the incident is said to have taken place during the exchange of vows or at the reception, but it usually occurs at the rehearsal dinner, one or two nights before the ceremony.

Imagine the jovial scene at the rehearsal dinner. Picture the bride and groom and everyone in the wedding party laughing and crying and hugging, sharing great stories over a terrific meal in the cozy back room of a popular restaurant. It's the kind of night that delivers memories for a lifetime.

After dinner, as the staff brings out clean plates for dessert, which will be served shortly, the bride wants to make an announcement.

"If I can just have everyone's attention for a moment," she says as she lightly taps her spoon against her glass.

The room grows quiet. This is an unusual and unexpected development, especially considering the bride's normally reserved demeanor. She's a shy girl who is not the type to give speeches unless it's absolutely necessary.

"First of all, I want to thank you all for coming," says the bride. "I know some of you have journeyed a long way to be at my wedding, and that will always mean a lot to me.

"There are some people I want to thank. First of all I'd like to express my gratitude to my parents for always being there for me. And my future in-laws, who have treated me like their own daughter from the moment I began dating their son.

"I'd also like to thank my brothers and sisters. I know I haven't always been the easiest person to live with, but I really do love you guys."

There are tears welling in the bride's eyes. Her mom and her grandmother are beginning to sniffle, as they beam proudly at their wonderful daughter. They know it's not easy for her to speak in front of a crowd, yet she ends up doing a wonderful job of easily expressing her emotions.

"Lastly," says the bride, "I want to thank my maid-of-honor, who has been my best friend for so long."

She turns to her best friend and continues: "That's right, thank you so much...for sleeping with my fiance!"

Grandma gasps in horror. The groom's father stands and bellows, "This is an outrage!" The groom says, "Honey, you're making a huge mistake." The maid of honor says, "What are you talking about?"

"You know damn well what I'm talking about," says the bride. "And if any of you doubt my word, why don't you take a look at the little surprise taped to the bottom of your dessert plates!"

With that, the bride runs out of the room, weeping, as everyone else turns over their plates and sees a graphic photo of the bride's best friend and her fiance making love. The bride had hired a private investigator to check out her suspicions about the two of them—suspicions that turned out to be all too true.

Needless to say, the wedding is called off, and the heartbroken bride never speaks again to her so-called best friend or her ex-fiance. The two cheating lovers eventually move out of town and get married to each other, but the union only lasted a couple of years before they were divorced.

Sometimes it's the groom who is the wronged party, as in this version that was posted on the Internet:

There was a huge wedding, with at least 400 guests. At the reception, the groom told the band to stop playing, and he jumped up on stage and grabbed the microphone. He's a funny guy who loves the spotlight, and everyone figured he'd tell some of his favorite jokes and thank everybody for coming.

"To show my appreciation to all of you, I've arranged it so that everyone here receives a special gift," he said. "If you'll reach under your chairs, you'll find a manila envelope taped to the bottom. I'd like everyone to find their envelope and then we'll open them together at the count of three, okay?"

There was much rustling and laughter as the 400 guests reached under their chairs and pulled out the hidden envelopes.

"All right, everybody ready?" said the groom. "Then here we go. One, two, three!"

First there was the sound of 400 envelopes ripping open. Then there was the sound of silence, as 400 people found themselves looking at photos of the bride and the best man in a compromising position. The groom had long suspected the bride and his best buddy of having an affair, and he had hired a private investigator to tail them. The photo had been taken just a week before the wedding.

The groom turned to the best man and said, "To hell with you. You can have her." Then he turned to the bride and said, "And to hell with you too. I want a divorce."

With that, he walked out of the reception hall.

☒ ☒ ☒

Fans of the daytime soap opera *The Bold and the Beautiful* saw yet another variation on this story in 1997. The character of Sally Spectra wanted to ruin the wedding of Eric and Stephanie, so she had her assistant Darla dress up as a caterer and sneak into the house where the wedding was to be held. Once she was safely inside, Darla slipped a photo of Sally and Eric into the minister's Bible.

At the service, the minister opened his Bible—and the incriminating photo tumbled out, for all to see.

"Maybe you'll want to talk about this first," said the minister.

The wedding was called off. As of this writing, Stephanie and Eric are still not back together.

I know. It's keeping me up nights, too.

The videotaped theft

These days, no wedding goes untaped, whether it's shot by a professional outfit or an uncle with his videocamera. Walk into any wedding reception in any banquet or dance hall in America, and you're sure to see at least one guy working the room like he's Martin Scorsese's cinematographer, sticking his camera in everyone's faces and interviewing people for the three hour-plus opus.

For all the hard work done by these would-be auteurs, who really wants to watch the final product? Wedding videos are only entertaining when awful or embarrassing behavior is caught on tape, when somebody's obnoxious 12-year-old nephew siphons a few ounces from Grandma's whiskey sour when she isn't looking, or the camera catches the groom's married brother cupping the rear end of a giggling bridesmaid, or you surreptitiously pick up a conversation at a table where they're making bets about how long the marriage will last.

Or, a thief is nabbed on tape, as in the following urban legend, which has been in circulation ever since the advent of the home videocam in the 1980s.

The scene is a reception in a popular banquet hall, with 300 guests celebrating the union of a fine, upstanding young couple. There's a table at the entrance for people to leave gifts, but most of the guests have come bearing envelopes containing cash or checks, and they hand these envelopes directly to the bride, who stuffs them into a silk bag which she leaves at her place setting as she mingles with guests.

"That's an awful lot of money to leave unattended," says her maid of honor, but the bride laughs and says, "Come on, it's a wedding, we know everybody here. It's not like someone's going to steal it."

She's right, the bag isn't stolen—but someone reaches in and steals the envelopes, replacing them with a bunch of envelopes containing nothing but strips of paper. Because the heft of the bag feels the same, the bride doesn't discover the shocking theft until well after the reception is over.

"There were 300 guests at that wedding, plus all the people who worked for the banquet hall," she says to her new husband. "We're *never* going to find out who did this!"

The next morning, before they leave for their honeymoon, they get a call from the groom's brother, who had spent the entire wedding running around with his video camera, shooting everything in sight.

"I was up all night watching the tape," he says. "You guys better come over. There's something you need to see." The couple hurries over to the guy's house, and he pops in the tape, with the video cued to the moment of truth.

"This was when everyone was on the dance floor for 'Celebration,'" he says. "Well, almost everyone. Look in the background, at the head table..."

As the bride and groom lean forward, the groom's brother hits the pause button and then begins to advance the tape frame by frame. A man in a tuxedo enters the picture and quickly removes the contents of the bride's bag, replacing them with the worthless, paper-stuffed envelopes.

"Oh my God," sobs the bride...for it's her very own father.

I've heard the "videotaped theft" story a dozen times, but it's always in the classic "friend of a friend" vein. No one has ever provided me with the names of any of the principals, let alone the chance to view the tape.

Wedding quickies

et's flip through the urban legend wedding photo album and gaze at a few snapshots of popular ULs about brides and grooms and wacky wedding guests.

The wrong *Robin Hood*

Kevin Costner's *Robin Hood: Prince of Thieves* was a box office hit that spawned a No. 1 hit record: "Everything I Do (I Do For You)" by the Canadian rocker Bryan Adams. It's one of those bombastic rock ballads that becomes a staple at proms, homecoming dances—and weddings. In fact, many a bride in the 1990's has asked that the song be played in lieu of the wedding march itself.

And so it was that a young bride told the church organist, a middle-aged fellow, of her desire for "the theme from *Robin Hood*" to be played as she walks down the aisle.

"But I'm not sure if that's appropriately dignified for such a solemn occasion," said the somewhat confused organist.

"Look, do you know the song?" said the bride.

"Well, sure, but—"

"But nothing. Just play it, okay? It's what I want. The theme from *Robin Hood*. Do you think you can handle that?"

The organist shrugged his shoulders. "If you insist."

"I insist."

On her wedding day, the bride never looked more beautiful. She stood at the back of the church, fighting the tears as she waited to hear the song she had specially chosen for the occasion...

The organist began to play—not the Bryan Adams song, but the bouncy, uptempo theme from the 1960 *Robin Hood* TV series:

Robin Hood, Robin Hood, riding through the glen...
Robin Hood, Robin Hood, with his band of merry men...

Titters erupted throughout the church. The bride frantically tried to signal to the organist that he was playing the wrong song, but he was so into it he never even looked up. She had no choice but to walk (rather, gallop) down the aisle as the cheesy adventure song blared through the church.

The X-rated couple

Another videotape caper. In this one, the couple has such a great time on their honeymoon that they return to the same resort—the same room, even—to celebrate their one-year anniversary. In order to get into the mood, they turn on the hotel's X-rated movie channel, and discover that they're the stars in the feature of the day! Someone had secretly videotaped them on their honeymoon, and their sexual antics had been duplicated and shown in a hundred hotels across the country.

Needless to say, the couple filed a major lawsuit and received a huge settlement.

The heel in the grate

Bridesmaid gets heel caught in wedding-aisle grate and leaves it there, her bare foot fortunately concealed by her long dress. Helpful groomsman tries to pry the shoe free, but he succeeds only in lifting the entire grate, with the heel still caught. Next up is the bride, who falls right through the opening and disappears.

This incident was re-created for the movie *The Glass-Bottom Boat* (but in a NASA training facility, not at a wedding.) Doris Day's heel gets caught in a grate, Rod Taylor picks up the grate with the shoe still attached, and Dick Martin (of Rowan & Martin fame) is the hapless sucker who falls into the hole.

Chapter Five
Rumors
in the
Air Tonight

Tupac Shakur is dead, but there's a growing cottage industry of theories and stories about why Tupac faked his death and is, in fact, alive and well, even recording under a *nom de rap*. We'll look at that nonsense here, along with a number of other popular urban myths about pop music, including the eerie origins of the Phil Collins hit, "In the Air Tonight."

A killer "In the Air Tonight"

With the possible exception of James Brown's "I Feel Good," perhaps no pop song in history has been used in as many commercials, TV shows, and movies as "In the Air Tonight" by Phil Collins. With its hypnotic opening, haunting lyrics, and percussion-driven crescendo, it's the perfect mood piece for any number of commercials or dramatic scenes.

I always figured "In the Air Tonight" was the story of a jealous man telling his lover he knows she's been unfaithful:

And I was there and I saw what you did, saw it with my own two eyes...

So you can wipe off that grin, I know where you've been...

It's all been a pack of lies.

And I can feel it coming in the air tonight...

In 1992, Collins was quoted in *Parade* as saying the song was about the breakup of his first marriage. Not that this rather ordinary explanation for the genesis (get it?) of "In the Air Tonight" did anything to dispel the long-running rumors about the *real* origin of the song. The details vary greatly from telling to telling, but the common theme is that Collins witnessed a death or tragedy of some great magnitude, and used that raw experience as material for the song. He then belted out "In the Air Tonight" in a passionate concert attended by the wrong-doer named in the song.

In one version, Collins is walking along the beach while his brother is out on Collins' boat. Some sort of accident occurs and Collins' brother falls overboard, but Collins is much too far away to do anything about it and his brother dies. The other boat speeds away without giving a statement to authorities, but Collins manages to catch the boat's name before it disappears from view. With the help of private detectives, he learns the identity of the boat captain.

He patiently waits a year, and then, with the help of a cooperative radio station and a friendly concert promoter, he fixes it so that the boat's owner "wins" 10th row tickets to see Collins live.

That night at the show, Collins says he's dedicating a new song, "In the Air Tonight," to his brother, who died tragically exactly one year ago. (He doesn't say how.) Halfway through the song, a spotlight shines directly on the boat captain, as Collins sings directly to him:

So you can wipe off that grin, I know where you've been...
It's all been a pack of lies!

The guilty fan realizes the song is about him, and he has a breakdown right then and there as the song kicks into its climax, with Collins furiously pounding the drums and the crowd going crazy.

In another version, the concert scenario is essentially the same—only this time the lucky winner isn't someone who didn't save Phil Collins' brother from drowning, it's a rapist or a killer who committed a crime while the singer looked on helplessly from a hidden spot nearby. Only when the thug hears the lyrics does he realize a famous songwriter has not only witnessed the crime but has set it to music. (Sometimes the rapist and/or killer's victim is Collins' own wife; sometimes it's a stranger.)

In yet another telling, Collins is mugged on the beach and chases the man into the water. The mugger gets caught in the undertow and cries out for help, but the famous singer stands by and does nothing. *Well if you told me you were drowning, I would not lend a hand, I've seen your face before my friend, but I don't know if you know who I am.* The song is supposedly about his own feelings of guilt over the mugger's death.

For the record, Phil Collins does not have a brother who drowned, nor was he the witness to some unspeakably horrible crime, nor did he refuse to help a sinking mugger. By all accounts, "In the Air Tonight" is about love gone wrong.

311 and the KKK

More than 40 years after Bill Haley & the Comets told us they wanted to rock around the clock, pop musicians still haven't run out of band names, although it's probably safe to say they've come close to exhausting the supply of *clever* band names. Some of today's groups have monikers that make you wonder if the band members didn't just get drunk and pick random words from a Scrabble dictionary or a can of alphabet soup.

Primitive Radio Gods. Goo Goo Dolls. Deep Blue Something. Mr. Fingers.

Then again, it's not as if things made any more sense in the era of the Strawberry Alarm Clock, Procol Harem, and Moby Grape.

Some groups actually do try to put a little meaning behind their names. Take 311, the raucous, dance-metal-hybrid rockers who got together in Omaha, Nebraska, and now make their home in Los Angeles. They were formed in 1990, and they've had a nice steady climb to national prominence: opening for Kiss, going gold with their third album (simply titled "311") and first hitting MTV with the single "Down."

Urban Legends

As soon as 311 started making national waves, speculation about the meaning of the band's name took off. In some interviews, they'd say that three minutes, 11 seconds was the perfect length for a hit single; often they'd joke that bass player P-Nut used to get a bill for $3.11 every time he went to Taco Bell. There was even the simple explanation that 3+1+1=5, which is the total number of members in the band.

But then *the* rumor started. The ugly one.

The letter "K" is the 11th letter in the alphabet, and some genius surmised that 311 meant the 11th letter three times in a row—KKK.

In 1996, the 311/KKK story was flying around Omaha's Westside High School, where three of the band members had attended school, and some students took their concerns to the administration. Just like that, 311 T-shirts were banned at the high school, as well as two other schools in the same district. Officials at Westside told the *Omaha World-Herald* that they took action after being told by the Omaha Police Department's gang unit that 311 was a reference to the Ku Klux Klan.

The ban attracted nationwide media attention: articles appeared in *USA Today*, *Rolling Stone*, and *Spin*; and there was a report on *MTV News*. Suddenly, 311 was getting more national press for its name than it ever had received for its music. The group's members were said to be distraught when they heard that some white supremacist organizations had become fans due to the supposed tribute to the KKK.

The actual origins of the name are much more benign. A former guitarist who played in an early version of the group was once caught skinny-dipping by the Omaha Police and was charged with indecent exposure—and the code on the ticket was 311.

As the rumors about the KKK continued to swirl, the band issued a statement on its web site

"It has come to our attention that there is a very unsettling rumor circulating regarding the name of our band 311. We have been told that certain white supremacist groups use the numbers 311 to represent KKK. This is a most unfortunate coincidence and one that is extremely disturbing to us. We would like to state for the record that this is completely at odds with our personal beliefs. We believe the only people worth hating are organized hate groups like the KKK. Anyone familiar with our lyrics know how we feel. Our lyrics make a strong stand against racism and a strong stand for positivity and unity. The name of our band originally comes from an Omaha police citation for indecent exposure. We thought it was funny at the time. Now our name simply means five friends from Omaha making music. Music that stands for peace and unity.

"Sincerely, 311"

Three years later, 311 is more popular than ever, but I've still heard the KKK story from young fans of the band. My advice: Change the name to The KKK Sucks, or go back to the original name, Fish Hippos (I'm not making that up), or get away from the controversy completely by going in another direction.

Perhaps the copyright on Strawberry Alarm Clock is available again.

Beatles reunite on *Saturday Night Live*

By the spring of 1976, it had been more than six years since the breakup of the Beatles, but John, Paul, George, and Ringo were still receiving a number of tremendously lucrative offers to reunite for an album, a reunion tour, or even a one-night concert. There were so many multimillion-dollar offers flying around that the hot new NBC show *Saturday Night Live* did a spoof in which producer Lorne Michaels appeared on camera flashing a check in the "generous amount of three thousand dollars," if the Beatles were to appear on the show. Michaels, keeping a straight face throughout the bit, said the money could be divided any way the Beatles saw fit: "If you want to give less to Ringo, that's fine."

The teenage daughter of a friend of mine recently asked me if it was true the Beatles accepted the offer and played on *Saturday Night Live* that year, and if so, was the video available? Silly as that question may have sounded, she was only repeating an advanced version of a story that had been circulating for two decades—namely, that at least two and maybe even three, of the Beatles tried to show up on the *SNL* stage the very night Michaels made the offer.

According to the legend, Paul McCartney was in New York that night, and he caught the broadcast on live television. John Lennon lived in New York and George Harrison also happened to be in town, and McCartney tracked both of them down and suggested they meet at Lennon's place, hop a taxi to the NBC studios, walk in and announce, "We're ready to play!"

Forgetting all the ugly spats that caused their breakup, the lads were reminded of the early days when such a prank would have seemed like the most natural thing in the world to do. Lennon and Harrison agreed to go along with the stunt, but it never played out because the taxi got caught in traffic and by the time the three former Beatles reached the studio, the show was over. They shook hands and went their separate ways, each one chuckling over the reunion that might have been.

🖾 🖾 🖾

A taxi? I don't think so. The boys would have found a more upscale form of transportation to whisk them to Rockefeller Plaza.

However, there is a thread of truth to this story, as John Lennon explained in the January 1981 edition of *Playboy*, shortly after Lennon was killed.

PLAYBOY: Aside from the millions you've been offered for a reunion concert, how did you feel about producer Lorne Michaels' generous offer of $3,200 [Author's note: Michaels had upped the offer in a later episode] for appearing on *Saturday Night Live* a few years ago?

LENNON:Oh, yeah. Paul and I were together watching that show. He was visiting us at our place at the Dakota. We were watching it and almost went down to the studio, just as a gag. We nearly got into a cab, but we were actually too tired...

PLAYBOY: How did you and Paul happen to be watching TV together?

LENNON: That was a period when Paul just kept turning up at our door with a guitar. I would let him in, but finally I said to him, "Please call before you come over. It's not 1956 and turning up at the door just isn't the same anymore. You know, just give me a ring." He was upset by that, but I didn't mean it badly. I just meant that I was taking care of a baby all day and some guy turns up at the door. But anyway, back on that night, he and Linda walked in and he and I were just sitting there, watching the show, and we went, "Ha-ha, wouldn't it be funny if we went down," but we didn't.

And so ended the silliest, last, and perhaps best opportunity for the two most important members of the Beatles to have shared the stage one last time.

The
Dave Matthews
chain letter

Every once in a while I'll read about a celebrity who likes to go online and anonymously surf around the Internet under one of those goofy AOL names like Muffy321 or Smelly874, maybe even visiting their own web sites, chat rooms, and message boards.

I can readily attest that it's an irresistible temptation; as a newspaper columnist and TV and radio commentator in Chicago, I've often been the subject of such discussion groups on the Internet, and I must admit I've visited those areas to see what people are saying. A couple of times I've even joined in the conversation, if only to set the record straight when I read something that is just plain incorrect. But even when I'm just lurking about, it's a strange sensation when you see that someone you've never met, someone who does not have to identify himself or herself in any way, can write something negative.

Imagine then what it must be like to be *really* famous, on a global level, and to have access to all these instant Internet conversations about your career, your love life, your family, etc. If a celebrity did respond to you, either via a direct e-mail or bulletin board posting, how would you know it wasn't an impostor? In the early days of the Internet, before most of the good log-ons were taken, anyone could have grabbed screen names such as Hanks222 or Elton432 and proclaimed themselves to be Tom Hanks or Elton John. Obviously, there was no way of knowing.

Be suspicious, then, if you receive an e-mail from singer/songwriter Dave Matthews. Over the last couple of years, Matthews (or, to be more accurate, somebody claiming to be him) has been a ubiquitous presence on the e-mail circuit with a letter that has been copied and forwarded thousands upon thousands of times.

I've had this sent to me at least a half-dozen times; in order to get to the text of the letter itself, I always have to scroll down past countless blocks of screen names and little attached messages imploring me to "Keep going, it's worth it!"

I also see a lot of notes like this:

SUBJECT: Fwd

Hey everybody, this is SO UNBELIEVABLY SAD! please read this and send it on to all your friends. if dave matthews can take the time so can you! a child's life could be at stake.

And:

SUBJECT: Help a dying kid!

Please keep scrolling and read the message at the bottom of this letter, it could save someone's life! this means you, all of you! don't let me down!

Finally, the letter itself:

Hi! This is Dave Matthews. That's right, Dave Matthews from the Dave Matthews Band. I want to thank everyone for supporting the band by buying our records and coming to see us in concert, but that's not why I'm writing to you today. No, this is something much more important, which is why I'm writing this myself. I just got America Online a while ago, and my secretary will send you my screen name if you send this to at least five more people who are online. The reason I am doing this is because a little girl needs our help and I thought I could use my fame to help out this sick little girl.

She has only six months to live, and as her dying wish she wanted to send a chain letter telling everyone to live their life to the fullest, since she never will. She'll never make it to the prom, she'll never graduate from high school, she'll never get married or have a family of her own. But by you sending this to as many people as possible, you can give her and her family a little hope, because with every name that this is sent to, the American Cancer Society will donate 3 cents per name to her treatment and recovery plan.

If you're too selfish or lazy to spend a few minutes forwarding this to a few of your friends, just remember: This could be you someday.

Your friend,

Dave Matthews

The chain letter, supposedly written by the rock star, contains exact fragments of other bogus fundraising E-mails authored by fictional cancer patients "Tamara Martin," "David Lawitts," and "Jessica Mydek" among others. It's also reminiscent of the Craig Shergold letter, examined earlier in this book. When you read the letter closely, you realize it makes little sense. First we're told the little girl is dying and she wants us all to appreciate our good fortune to be healthy. Then we're told if we pass on the letter, a donation will be made to assist in her "treatment and recovery."

Not to mention the fact that the American Cancer Society is not in the business of doling out money for treatment based on who gets the most "hits" on the Internet. Says Bud Jones, vice president of communications and government affairs for the organization: "The American Cancer Society is not in the business of giving away money. None of this is true. In fact the Dave Matthews rumor is a variation on a theme. There's a new one cropping up lately about a doctor writing a similar letter about a kid and sending it around. The doctor named in the letter is an actual person, but when we contacted him, he said he had nothing to do with the letter."

The
surprise
guest guitarist

I f you put all the great reviews Grand Funk Railroad
ever received in a scrapbook, it would be about as
thick as a takeout menu from your favorite restaurant.
In the 1970s, long-haired lead singer Mark Farner and
his bandmates sold millions of albums and churned out
numerous hits such as "We're an American Band," "I'm
Your Captain/Closer to Home," and a remake of Little
Eva's "Locomotion", but they were almost unanimously
dismissed by critics and rock purists as a hack band playing to the lowest common denominator.

That's why Grand Funk Railroad is the perfect group
to star in a popular urban legend. Seems the band was
playing to a packed house sometime around 1972, and
everyone in the crowd was going crazy—with one notable exception. The boys were distracted by the constant booing and heckling coming from a lone male voice
in front of the stage.Finally, the lead guitarist grabbed
the microphone between songs and said, "We're trying
to do a show up here, but someone is hassling us. Tell
you what: If you think you can do better, why don't you
come on up here?"

"As a matter of fact I think I will!" bellows the man.

The guys in the band can't really see what's going on because of the spotlights in their eyes, but there's a great commotion as the unknown heckler makes his way to the stage and is helped up by a couple of roadies. "Can you believe the guy's actually coming up here?" says Farner.

When the heckler steps into the light, a roar of recognition surges through the crowd.

It's none other than Eric Clapton.

In January of 1997, a variation on this story was retold on the Internet:

"One night, sometime around 1970, Grand Funk had 'em packed into Detroit's Cobo Arena, but for some reason, they just couldn't connect with the audience. As they cranked out each hit, the boos got louder and louder until Mark Farner screamed at the audience, 'If anybody out there can play guitar better than me, they can just come up here and do it!'

"Quietly, a solitary figure stepped out of the crowd, and, head bowed, made his way onto the stage. As the security guards stepped aside, he walked up to Farner, who immediately unstrapped his guitar and gave it to him. The stranger, now in the spotlight, strummed one chord and said, 'Hello, I'm Eric Clapton.'

"Grand Funk slinked off the stage and turned it over to Clapton, who played solo to a manic crowd for the next two hours."

Sometimes the band in the story is the Guess Who instead of Grand Funk Railroad, but the heckling musician has always been identified as Clapton. Why Eric

Clapton would be at a Grand Funk Railroad or Guess Who concert in the first place is anybody's guess, but it's safe to assume that even the Clapton of those crazy days wouldn't have been so rude as to heckle a mid-level band, nor choose to take over a concert and play for free.

Clapton's incredible guitar skills play a factor in another urban legend, in which the local pastor at a church in England politely rebuffs young Eric's offer to play some acoustic guitar during Sunday Mass, finally relenting only because he feels sorry for the lad. When Clapton does get his chance, he's beyond great, of course.

The Clapton story has also morphed into an oft-told tale about a young comic who goes on *The Tonight Show* or the *Late Show with David Letterman* and tells a story about his most embarrassing moment onstage. Seems he was playing the Comedy Store one night and was getting a pretty good response from the audience, with the exception of one clown who kept stepping on his punch lines. The comic was of course blinded by the spotlight, but he started bantering with the heckler until he ran out of material and said in exasperation, "Look, if you think you're so funny, why don't you come up here and I'll sit in the audience?"

"Don't mind if I do!" replied the unruly customer—who turned out to be none other than Robin Williams.

Or Eddie Murphy, as I've heard it told elsewhere.

UL FOOTNOTE. This story was chronicled by the *Chicago Tribune* and was confirmed by dozens of eyewitnesses. Some years ago, a pickup basketball game on the south side of Chicago was interrupted by a brash talker who wanted a piece of the action. In this instance, though, there was no mistaking the heckler. It was Michael Jordan, who played in a couple of spirited games with the talented street kids and then sped off in his car. Jordan also regularly participated in pickup games in some of the more exclusive downtown health clubs in Chicago, and those who played against him said he was as competitive in a game of half-court hoops with a bunch of amateurs as he was in the NBA finals.

"You Oughta Know" who this song's about

A lanis Morissette, the former teenage actor from Canada, exploded onto the music scene in 1995 with the release of her third album, *Jagged Little Pill*, which has sold more than 20 million copies worldwide. The first single, "You Oughta Know," was a savage, bitter story of a young woman who lashes out at her ex-boyfriend for quickly finding a new lover.

Did you forget about me, Mister Duplicity?
I hate to bug you in the middle of dinner...
It was a slap in my face how quickly I was re-placed...
Are you thinking of me when you f**k her?

"You Oughta Know" has been the subject of much speculation about whether or not the song has a real-life inspiration. In a 1995 interview with the *Toronto Sun*, the 21-year-old Morissette acknowledged the existence of such a muse.

"I haven't heard from him," she told the paper. "And I don't think he knows. Which sort of says a lot about him. The ironic thing is, if anybody questions whether it's them I'm writing about, that means something in and of itself. People who were kind and honest and full of integrity throughout the process of making this album wouldn't question whether they were in that song because they would know."

Two male celebrities have been pegged as the man referenced in "You Oughta Know": Bob Saget, and Dave Coulier of *Full House* fame.

I've heard from a few Morissette fans who swear Saget is the ex-boyfriend targeted in the song. But they've got it mixed up. The Coulier theory is certainly much more plausible.

"It wasn't Bob Saget. It was that other guy on *Full House*, the one who was funny and had blond hair," posted one fan on the Internet. "He was on a radio station in Boston and admitted for the first time that he was the person Alanis sang about in her song. He got some girl pregnant while he was dating her."

Another post:

" 'You Oughta Know' was written about Dave Coolea [*sic*]...from *Full House*. They used to date, then he dumped her. I heard this straight from his mouth on K-ROQ [on the] Kevin and Bean morning show. They found it out, called him, and he confirmed it's all true!"

The weird thing is, Morissette really did date Coulier. In the early 1990s, when she was fairly well known in Canada because of her work on the series *You Can't do That on Television* and her pop career, Morissette was hired by the NHL's new franchise, the Ottawa Senators, to entertain the crowds. That led to her being asked to sing "O Canada" at the 1992 NHL All-Star game in Montreal. It was there that she met Coulier, a rabid hockey fan and amateur player who often participated in charity games. The relationship reportedly ended because at 19, Morissette felt she was too young to start a family.

Cut to a few years later, when "You Oughta Know" topped the charts. Morissette was now recast as the quintessential angry young woman, thrashing about the stage as she sang about the man who left her for another woman. This led to much speculation about the identity of the man in the song. Among those mentioned were Mike Peluso of the Ottawa Senators, and *Friends* star Matt LeBlanc, who appeared in a Morissette video before she became a big star.

Leslie Howe, a longtime Morissette friend and sometime collaborator, was so upset that his name was bandied about that he called the *Ottawa Star* to deny he was the inspiration for the song. "Alanis and I were friends and worked together professionally," he told the paper. "But we certainly never dated."

But the name mentioned most often is Dave Coulier's. In Paul Cantin's biography, *Alanis Morissette*, the singer says this about the rumor: "I'm not going to deny or say yes to it because I think it is wrong. I sort of laugh at it. That was a most public relationship, and it is a predictable answer...The truth is I am never going to tell who it is about." Cantin quotes Morissette as saying it would be unnecessarily cruel to reveal the identity of the man in the song. "If it was written for the sake of revenge, Lord knows, I would be plastering his picture everywhere. And I would never do that, because I have too much respect for him."

The E! website tries to refute the Coulier story: "Although [Coulier] still likes to think of himself as the muse who sparked Morissette, that place in history is reserved for another old Canuck boyfriend."

The dark side of Oz

As with the great majority of urban legends, it's impossible to determine exactly when this one started, but we can surmise with some confidence *how* it got started. Somebody was really stoned, and they popped in Pink Floyd's *Dark Side of the Moon* on the stereo while *The Wizard of Oz* began playing on the VCR. Our unknown stoner/scholar takes a massive hit on his bong and settles back into his bean bag chair for a multi-sensory experience. As the MGM lion roars, side one of *Dark Side of the Moon* begins. At first the viewer doesn't notice anything strange, but as the movie and the music play on, he gets an eerie feeling: They're somehow synchronized!

The parallels are too accurate and too often to be attributed to mere coincidence. In chronological order, here are some of the connections:

♦ In one of the opening scenes, Dorothy is looking at the ground as we hear the words, "look around and choose your ground."

♦ Dorothy opts not to sit on a bench as we hear the words, "Don't sit down..."

- A synthesizer that sounds like an airplane is heard on *Dark Side of the Moon* at the precise moment when Dorothy is looking at the sky.

- We hear bells on the album at the exact moment when Margaret Hamilton rides in on her bicycle, ringing the bike's bell.

- Dorothy is seen running just as the band sings, "No one told you when to run..."

- During the song "Pulse," a woman's voice can be heard whispering very softly. Crank up the volume and you'll hear what she's saying: "I never said I was afraid of Dorothy."

- When the tornado plunks Dorothy into Munchkin Land and the screen changes from black-and-white to color, the cash registers of "Money" kick in. This is a sly reference to the Yellow Brick Road, and its bricks of gold.

- As the Good Witch's bubble enters the picture, we hear the words "goody good bulls**t."

- When the Wicked Witch makes her first appearance, we hear the words, "black, black."

- During the song "Us and Them," we hear the words "and who knows which is which and who is who" just as Dorothy is confused, trying to figure out which of these bizarre characters are the good guys and which ones are dangerous.

- The first time we see the Scarecrow, "Brain Damage" starts playing. The Scarecrow is dancing as we hear the words, "The lunatic is on the grass."

- Dorothy and the Scarecrow are about to enter the dark forest as we hear the words, "See you on the dark side of the moon..."

- The heartbeat sound effect heard at the end of the

album kicks in just as Dorothy is beating on the Tin Man's chest.

End of album. But obviously the movie isn't over, which is one of the problems with this urban legend. *Dark Side of the Moon* has a running time less than half that of *The Wizard of Oz*, but some of the "Pink Freud" legends I've heard continue to draw comparisons between sections of the album and scenes from the film right until the moment when Dorothy returns home. What are you supposed to do—re-cue the album?

That's another serious flaw in this admittedly entertaining theory. In 1973, when *Dark Side of the Moon* was recorded, the only copies of *The Wizard of Oz* available would have been theatrical prints. While it's theoretically possible that Roger Waters, David Gilmour, and company could have arranged to have a print of the film playing while they composed the album, such a complicated feat would be much easier in the modern era of videocassettes, laser discs, DVDs, and digital technology. To attempt to synchronize an album to the flickering images on a silver screen would seem to be a nearly impossible task, even for the creative geniuses of Pink Floyd.

As far as I was able to determine, none of the notoriously media-shy members of Floyd have ever commented on this urban legend, which didn't surface until about two decades after the album was released. However, rock scholar Timothy White, the author of the definitive biography of the band, says there's absolutely no truth to the story.

In the interest of research, I forced myself to watch *The Wizard of Oz* again with the sound turned down and a CD of *Dark Side of the Moon* cued up. I don't smoke dope but I do drink Red Stripe beer, and I sipped a couple just to get into a more accepting mood. Weirdly enough, most of the episodes described above actually did occur, and I have to admit I got the chills a couple of times, like when Dorothy knocked on the Tin Man's chest and a heartbeat comes out of the CD player. We can chalk up some of these Floyd/Oz parallels to coincidence and others to wishful thinking on the part of the interpreters, but the whole thing is a bit freaky.

You also have to figure it's a matter of time before some gimmick-hungry group deliberately records an album that meshes with a popular movie, whether it be *The Wizard of Oz* or something more contemporary. Tell me you wouldn't sell a billion copies of your record if word got out that it was a "secret soundtrack" to something like *Star Wars* or *Titanic*.

The "Love Rollercoaster" death scream

When I was about 14, some of my favorite albums in the whole world came from the funky rhythm and soul group known as the Ohio Players. Along with groundbreaking bands such as Sly & the Family Stone; Earth, Wind & Fire; and Kool & the Gang, they produced a kind of *Soul Train*-meets-Big-Band sound that was perfect for the era.

Their biggest hit of all was "Love Rollercoaster," the 1975 release that sailed to the top of the Billboard charts. I remember listening to "Love Rollercoaster" in somebody's basement when a buddy of mine told a hair-raising story about the recording of the song—in particular, the musical bridge where you hear a twanging guitar and what sounds like a woman screaming.

"Someone gave the producer an audio tape of a woman actually being murdered, and he thought it would be cool to put it in the song," my pal claimed. "The Ohio Players didn't know this; they just thought some actress had done the recording. By the time they learned the truth it was too late—the song was already playing on the radio. In protest, they said they would never play the song in concert or on TV shows such as *Soul Train*."

In college several years later, I heard another take on the "Love Rollercoaster" death scream. "The Ohio Players got a tape recording of a woman falling to her death on the Blue Streak rollercoaster ride in Cedar Point Amusement Park in Ohio, and they used it on the song," I was told.

More preposterous was the notion that the scream "accidentally" showed up on the song. Supposedly the band recorded the song in guitarist/vocalist Jimmy "Sugarfoot" Bonner's apartment, and a murder took place next door. The scream was recorded by the sound engineers, the band isolated the sound and increased the volume, and they kept it on the record because it perfectly fit the song.

Even the naked woman from the *Honey* album cover was brought into the legend. In the cover photo, she's kneeling atop a sheet of Fiberglass; according to the UL, when the honey on her body connected with the synthetic material, it became as sticky as Superglue, and her skin was spontaneously fused to the sheet. The act of ripping her legs free created terrible abrasions, and she was scarred for life, thus ruining her career as a nude model. Several weeks later, the Ohio Players were doing some mixing on "Love Rollercoaster" when the hysterical model burst through the door of the recording studio with a gun and threatened to kill them for destroying her livelihood. Before she could get off any shots, the band's manager stabbed her to death. The mikes were on and tape was rolling during this confrontation, and the woman's final screams of anguish were used on the record.

Nearly a quarter-century after "Love Rollercoaster" was released, the myth got a boost from the movie *Urban Legend*. In the movie, a bunch of college kids who weren't even born when "Love Rollercoaster" came out are playing it at a party, and a guy tries to impress a chick by telling her the UL about the song.

Guy: Listen. That scream. That's an actual cry for help by a girl being murdered.

Girl: You're kidding me.

Guy: No! That's why it sounds so real, because it was lifted of a 911 tape.

Girl: That's great.

The truth is that the scream comes from a vocalist who was simply trying to hit the highest note possible, emulating what it might sound like if someone were on a really scary rollercoaster. The best explanation for the whole "death scream" rumor was that it was apparently started by some long-forgotten DJ who made a joke about it back in 1975, and it's taken on a life of its own ever since. As Ohio Player drummer Jimmy "Diamond" Williams once said, "People were asking us, 'Did you kill this chick in the studio?' The band took a vow of silence because that makes you sell more records."

But listening to a digitally remastered recording of "Love Rollercoaster" through headphones, I have to admit the hairs on my arm stood up when I heard that scream. Maybe it's the resonance of the woman's voice, maybe it's the way the scream was mixed in, maybe it's the accumulation of all those stories over the years, but it sure gave me the creeps.

Is Tupac alive?

We love our pop stars so much we don't want to let them go. Elvis would be the most famous example, of course. Even though the guy was a study in excess, his legions of worshippers cling to the desperate hope that somewhere on this planet he continues to live.

Elvis died because he abused himself into oblivion. Little did he know his death would spawn a huge cult of true believers who to this day decorate their homes with images of him.

In 1996, the famed rap star Tupac Shakur joined Elvis in the next world—and he soon became the subject of more "he's alive!" conjecture then the King himself. Within days of Tupac's death, I was hearing from rap fans who implored me to ignore the hype and tell the "real story," i.e., Tupac wasn't dead at all, he was just hiding.

What occurred was that on Sept. 7, 1996, the rapper was in a car on East Flamingo Road in Las Vegas with Marion "Suge" Knight, the chairman of Death Row Records, when they were ambushed by an assailant who fired off more than a dozen shots. Shakur was struck four times in the chest and abdomen, while Knight sustained only minor injuries.

Six days later, Shakur died in a Las Vegas Hospital. He was 25 years old.

End of story—beginning of conspiracy theory.

Thousands of Tupac fans cling to the belief that their man faked his own death as a way of preserving his life. Rivals were closing in on him and he knew they were going to try to take him out, so he staged his own execution and disappeared.

On Feb. 19, 1999, *Nightline* devoted its entire program to the cult of Tupac. Chris Wallace, filling in for Ted Koppel, said in the show's introduction, "[Shakur's] music provided a voice for a lot of people who don't feel anyone's listening to them. They call him their poet, even their prophet, and more than two years after his murder, some of them still don't want to let go."

The program also makes mention of some of the web sites devoted to proving Tupac is still alive. These sites often include lists of "reasons to believe Tupac is alive," which include the following clues and arguments:

1. Tupac died on a Friday the 13th, "a very superstitious and suspicious day throughout history."

2. Because he had survived a previous shooting and was the subject of numerous death threats, Tupac almost always wore a bulletproof vest when he went out.

3. Suge Knight refused to cooperate with the investigation into Tupac's death. Maybe that's because there wasn't really a shooting that resulted in a fatality.

4. In the song "Life Goes On," Tupac raps about his own funeral.

5. In the video, "I Ain't Mad at 'Cha," released shortly after his death, Tupac portrays an angel in heaven. He's shot in the video while leaving a theater with a friend.

6. Just before his so-called death, Tupac changed his name to Makavali—a reference to the Italian strategist Machiavelli, who in his writings suggested one should fake one's death in order to gain advantage over one's enemies.

7. Why was Tupac cremated the day after he died? What were they trying to cover up?

8. Tupac died at 4:03 p.m. Four plus three equals seven. Tupac was 25. Two plus five equals seven. Seven, of course, is a lucky number. Was Tupac sending a message to his fans, telling them he was really "lucky," in other words, alive?

9. More numerology involving that lucky number: Tupac was shot on the 7th of the month. There were 12 shots fired, with five hits. Twelve minus five equals seven. Tupac's birthday is the 16th. One plus six equals seven. On the song "White Man's World," you can hear a voice whispering, "Seven years, seven years, seven years..."

10. In the video for "I Wonder if Heaven Got a Ghetto," the clock in the diner says "4:03," the time of Tupac's death.

11. In the first three seconds of the song "Seven Day Theory," you can hear the words, "Suge shot me" very softly. Suge was in the car with Tupac. Is this Tupac's way of saying Suge was in on the conspiracy?

12. On the song "Ain't 2 Hard to Find," Tupac raps, "I heard rumors that I died, murdered in cold blood, traumatized, pictures of me in my final states, you know mama cried, but that was fiction, some coward got the story twisted..."

13. In the "Toss It Up" video, Tupac is wearing a brand of Penny Hardaway Nikes that weren't available before his death!

14. A man who bears a striking resemblance to Tupac has been hanging around the poetry scene near Howard University in Washington. The man goes by the name of Juice, which was the name of Tupac's character in the movie *Poetic Justice.*

I just realized I provided 14 clues to suggest Tupac is alive. Fourteen divided by two equals...*seven!*

The numerology nonsense aside, I'd like to refute the Tupac-is-alive theory with one argument of my own:

1. Tupac got shot four times at close range, and members of his family identified the body.

Other chart topping legends

Without commercial interruptions, let's play some other music-related urban legends back to back to back:

The *Bat Out of Hell* will

Millions of fans think Meat Loaf's multi-platinum album *Bat Out of Hell*, featuring the over-the-top classics "Two Out of Three Ain't Bad" and "Paradise By the Dashboard Light," is right up there with the Beatles' *White Album*, Led Zeppelin *IV* and The Who's *Tommy* as one of the greatest albums in the history of rock.

Millions of others think it's worse than Muzak in a supermarket on a Saturday afternoon.

From such loathing springs the urban legend about the eccentric millionaire who dies and has it put in his will that his chief beneficiary, who apparently hates Meat Loaf, must listen to *Bat Out of Hell* in its entirety *every day for the rest of his life*, or he won't receive his monthly inheritance check.

One question: Who was supposed to monitor the beneficiary's behavior every day to make sure he listened to the album? For the monitor's sake, I hope he *loves* Meat Loaf.

"Hey hey wefe the Mansons"?

As you probably know, the infamous mass murderer Charles Manson was a would-be musician who recorded a number of demo songs and even lived for a time with Beach Boys drummer Dennis Wilson. Tinny-sounding Manson recordings occasionally are played by "controversial" DJs who want to show how outrageous they can be. In that same vein, rockers Guns 'N' Roses included a Manson song on their album *The Spaghetti Incident*.

Manson desperately wanted success as a pop singer. He even auditioned to be on *The Monkees* TV show—or so the UL goes.

In 1965, *Variety* ran an advertisement from producers Bob Rafelson and Bert Schneider, who were looking for "four insane boys, aged 17-21," to audition for a new TV series about an American version of a Beatlesque band, The Monkees. There were more than 400 respondents, including a young Stephen Stills, who didn't make the final cut. A clean-cut Manson was also reportedly among the would-be musicians hoping *The Monkees* would be his big break, but Manson (like Stills and future stars Harry Nilsson and Danny Hutton of Three Dog Night) was deemed to be not quite as talented as Mickey Dolenz, Mike Nesmith, Peter Tork, and Davey Jones. No wonder he went crazy.

This has become an accepted part of Manson lore, repeated on radio shows and TV shows, and cited as fact in newspaper articles. To wit, a *Chicago Tribune* article from Feb. 19, 1999, about an offbeat theater group doing a musical based on Manson's life, includes this background information on Manson's colorful insanity: "He hung out with Dennis Wilson of the Beach Boys [who allegedly wanted to become part of the Manson family], tried to get Terry Melcher—Doris Day's record-producing son—to make him a star, actually auditioned for *The Monkees* TV show, thought he heard prophesies about a genocidal race war in The Beatles' lyrics on *The White Album*, and thought he was Jesus Christ."

Everything there is true—except the Monkees thing. The problem with this story is that it's simply not possible. In 1965, Manson was serving time in the penitentiary at McNeil Island in Washington state, for parole violation. He wasn't released until the spring of 1967, long after *The Monkees* was already on the air.

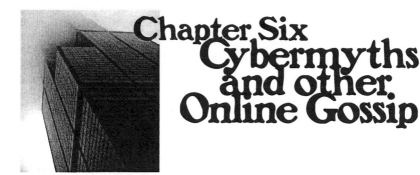

Chapter Six
Cybermyths and other Online Gossip

O ld-fashioned chain letters are mildly annoying, but there's something almost quaintly charming about the way they circulate around the world, compared with the annoying, staccato, rapid-fire avalanche of chain faxes and E-mails we now receive on almost a daily basis at work or home. With a few taps of the keyboard, some well-meaning friend or associate will send us yet another heavily-forwarded message warning us about some under-publicized danger, advertising a non-existent giveaway, or informing us of the latest tricky virus making the rounds

Nike shoe rebate

Most old gym shoes are nothing more than smelly fodder for the dumpster, but some well-worn Nike relics are rare treasures worth big bucks on the open market. If you've got an original pair of Air Jordans from the mid-1980s, for example, there are people in Japan willing to pay handsomely to take them off your hands. This is a true fact from the kinky world of collectibles, a world where Mark McGwire's 70th home run ball is valued at $3 million and cookie jars owned by Andy Warhol can sell for $1,000 and up.

Even more mundane pairs of old Nikes can serve a purpose, as the image-conscious company has figured out a way to recycle the rubber from those old shoes into material that can be turned into playground surfaces and basketball courts. Nike collects old gym shoes of all brands and makes them into a material called Nike Grind that is used for "new playgrounds, tennis courts, basketball courts, and running tracks," according to Nike's web site.

This recycling program undoubtedly was the root of the Internet urban legend about a "rebate" offer from Nike that seemed too good to be true.

A typical e-mail:

Just a quick note to tell you about a program that Nike started to help make fields and programs for the underprivileged from old tennis shoes. All YOU have to do is send in your old tennis shoes (NO MATTER WHAT THEY LOOK LIKE) with a piece of paper that has your name and address on it, and Nike will send you a brand new pair FREE OF COST!!!!* The tennis shoes you send DO NOT have to be Nike, just as long as they are tennis shoes. It really is a worthwhile project, and it's helping a lot of young kids.

Here is the address:

Nike Recycling Center
c/o Reuse a Shoe
26755 SW 95th Street
Wilsonville, OR 97070

Otherwise you are just going to throw them out and they go to waste. This way someone can get some use out of them. Nike really does send you a BRAND NEW pair of shoes even if you send in K-Swiss. Pass this to anyone and everyone you know so everyone can help out.

You'll notice a pattern in the texts of these e-mail chain letters—they almost always read as if penned by junior high students who are attempting to imitate adults, e.g., "Otherwise you are just going to throw them out and they go to waste." You'd think someone would elevate the grammar and clean up the syntax as the e-mail gets passed from computer to computer, but there seems to be an unwritten law of etiquette that says the original message should not be touched as it's passed along.

Like most companies plagued by Internet hoaxes, Nike decided it was better to address the issue than to ignore it and hope it would fade away. Under the typically immodest headline, "NIKE EXPOSES INTERNET HOAX," the company released a statement that read, in part:

BEAVERTON, OR—Internet users who are receiving and responding to e-mail messages purportedly from Nike are the unwitting victims of a hoax. Several variations are being spread across cyberspace, all claiming offers that seem too good to be true. They aren't.

"Nike never sends unsolicited e-mails over the Internet," said Scott Reames, Nike Corp. communications director. "We do not condone these e-mail hoaxes, and are dismayed that well-intentioned people are being duped into wasting their time."

Reames touched on something that is sure to be explored in surveys and studies for years to come—the amount of time wasted by people who spread rumors and/or respond to bogus offers on the Internet.

"If Nike were to make any sort of offer to consumers over the Internet, it would not be via unsolicited chain e-mails," said the company's press release.

UL ADVICE. If you receive an e-mail with more than three exclamation points at the end of a sentence, you can be almost 100 percent sure you're dealing with a hoax!!!!!

Blacks losing
the right
to vote

The first time I heard of this disturbing urban legend was when I got a call from an African-American reader in the summer of 1998.

"Did you know blacks are going to lose the right to vote in the year 2007?" he said.

"That's crazy," I said. "What are you talking about?"

"You've got to look into this and write about it," he said. "You've got to get the word out! Remember when Lyndon Johnson signed the Voting Rights Act in the 1960s?"

"I don't remember it because I was about five at the time," I said, "but I know what you're talking about."

"Well, the key word in the Voting Rights Act is 'act.' I got an e-mail today explaining that the Johnson legislation was an act, not an amendment. Reagan signed a 25-year extension of the Voting Rights Act in 1982, but that expires in 2007, and blacks will no longer have the right to vote unless somebody does something about it now."

The story sounded ridiculous—after all, blacks had the right to vote long before Johnson was in office—but I promised the caller I'd look into it.

Within days of that call, I received three or four e-mail affirmations of what I'd already discovered on my own—I was dealing with a burgeoning urban legend.

An edited version of the e-mail:

PLEASE PASS THIS ON TO AS MANY PEOPLE AS YOU CAN!!!!!!

Do you know the significance of the year 2007 to Black America? Did you know our right to vote will expire that year? This is no joke.

The Voting Rights Act signed by Lyndon B. Johnson was just an ACT. It was not made into LAW. In 1982 Ronald Reagan amended the Voting Rights Act for only another 25 years. Which means that in year 2007 we could lose the right to vote!

Blacks are the only group of people who still require PERMISSION under the United States Constitution to vote! In the year 2007 Congress will once again convene to decide whether blacks should have the right to vote. In order for this to be passed, 38 states will have to approve another extension.

We must contact our elected representatives to put a stop to this extension madness, and to urge them to make it LAW that blacks have the right to vote.

We have come too far to let the government make us grovel for the right to vote. Please pass this on to all black brothers and sisters, and all our non-black brothers and sisters who are true Americans and support equality for EVERYONE.

We'll let the U.S. Department of Justice clarify things, in excerpts from their official statement responding to this rumor:

"The Department of Justice has received numerous inquiries concerning a rumor that has been intermittently circulating around the nation for many months. According to this rumor, the Voting Rights Act will expire in 2007, and as a result African Americans are in danger of losing the right to vote that year.

"The rumor is false. The voting rights of African Americans are guaranteed by the United States Constitution and the Voting Rights Act, and those guarantees are permanent and do not expire. The 15th amendment to the Constitution [*which was ratified in 1870—author's note]* and the Voting Rights Act of 1965 prohibit racial discrimination in voting. Under the 15th amendment and the Voting Rights Act, no one may be denied the right to vote because of his or her race or color...

"The basic prohibition against discrimination in voting contained in the 15th amendment and in the Voting Rights Act does not expire in 2007— in fact, it does not expire at all, it is permanent."

It is true that the some elements of Voting Rights Act will expire in 2007—but these items were never intended to be in effect forever.Unfortunately, there were special circumstances that led to the creation of the Voting Rights Act in the first place. For decades, blacks in the South had been harassed, threatened, assaulted, and otherwise prohibited from exercising their Constitutional right to vote. The civil rights movement led to the Voting Rights Act, which spelled out "special provisions containing extraordinary remedies," as the government put it, for a limited time period applying to specific areas where blacks were not allowed to vote

The act was scheduled to expire after five years, but it was extended in 1970 by Richard Nixon, in 1975 by

Gerald Ford, and in 1982 by Ronald Reagan. No doubt whoever's in charge in 2007 will once again extend the legislation, if only for public relations purposes. Even if the special provisions section of the Voting Rights Act was allowed to expire, those provisions can be reinstated by court order if there's evidence of discriminatory practices in a particular region. And with or without the act, the 15th amendment guaranteeing all citizens of legal age the right to vote is permanent and binding.

Still, the rumor was so dominant on the Internet that in December of 1998, the *Associated Press* ran a story about it.

"[W]hat is distressing to so many black leaders is that so many black people would give even a second thought to [the] claim that their voting rights will expire in 2007, when certain provisions of the Voting Rights Act run out unless renewed by Congress," the story says. Rep. James Clyburn (D.-S.C.) told the AP his office was receiving "hundreds of calls" about the rumor. "It's frustrating dealing with this hoax," he said.

🔯 🔯 🔯

I'm thinking of sending out an e-mail of my own:

"URGENT! Millions of people don't understand how the Constitution works! They're needlessly spreading rumors about blacks losing the right to vote!"

Think anyone will fall for that?

Bill Gates teams up with Disney

That Bill Gates sure is a benevolent billionaire, isn't he? Seems like every time I surf the Net I'm learning about another generous giveaway, courtesy of the bespectacled founder of Microsoft. It's a wonder he has time to oversee new product development, what with all the time he spends composing e-mail messages to the masses.

Maybe that's why Gates teamed up with Walt Disney Jr. in 1998 on a giveaway opportunity. He probably figured he could save time and enhance his image by hooking up with another famous and widely respected brand name.

This message was flying all over the Internet in the summer of '98:

WALT DISNEY JR. GREETING

Hello Disney fans:

And thank you for signing up for Bill Gates' E-Mail tracking. My name is Walt Disney Jr. Here at Disney we are working with Microsoft which has just completed an E-mail tracing program that tracks everyone to whom this message is forwarded to. It does through an unique IP (Internet Protocol) address log book database.

We are experimenting with this and need your help. Forward this to everyone you know and if it reaches 13,000 people, 1,300 of the people will receive $5,000, and the rest will receive a free trip for two to Disney World for one week during the summer of 1999 at our expense.

Enjoy.

Your friends,
Walt Disney Jr., Disney, Bill Gates and the Microsoft Development Team

"There is no Walt Disney Jr.," a Disney spokesman told me. "Walt didn't have any sons, he had daughters. There was a Roy Disney Jr., but of course he wasn't Walt's son, he was Roy Disney's son."

The lack of a Walt Disney Jr. is just one solid piece of evidence that this thing is totally bogus. All this computer-talk about "e-mail tracking applications" and "IP address log book databases" is beyond silly. Microsoft is one of the most sophisticated and powerful companies in the world; does anyone really believe the phantom Walt Disney Jr., along with Bill Gates "and the Microsoft Development Team" would have to reach out to strangers on the Internet with a chain letter in order to test any kind of program?

The Disney-Gates letter is actually a spinoff of an earlier hoax, supposedly from Gates alone, in which he solicits help with his company's new e-mail tracing program and offers "$1,000 and a copy of Windows98 at my expense" to the first 1,000 people who responded. My newspaper, the *Chicago Sun-Times*, contacted

Microsoft in February of 1998 to get a response to Gates' solo offer. The company responded with a statement: "This message did not come from Mr. Gates. There is no such program and no such offer is being made to our customers. Someone is playing a bad joke."

A month later, Gates himself wrote an op-ed piece for the *New York Times* in which he felt it necessary to address the problem.

"[M]y name was recently attached to a hoax e-mail message that was widely distributed," Gates wrote. "People embellished the fraudulent e-mail over time, as it was forwarded from electronic mailbox to electronic mailbox...

"Well, it is hooey. There is a lot of hooey on the Internet, and a lot that's rude. But that doesn't mean that the Internet isn't wonderful, that it won't change the world or that it won't get a lot better over time..."

You see that? Even while attempting to crush a pesky rumor involving his good name, Bill Gates reminds us all what a wonderful place the Internet can be.

But even the richest man in the world was unable to quell the urban legend. Just when the "Bill Gates $1,000 giveaway" rumor started dying down, the combo-platter offer from Gates and good old Walt Disney Jr. surfaced. There's no shortage of computer-literate pranksters who get a big kick out of tweaking Mr. Gates, in the process giving false hope to thousands of bored individuals who peruse an e-mail about a possible free trip to Disney World and immediately begin dreaming of escaping to Orlando for a week.

Shannon's internet lesson

I wish I could give credit to the author of this cautionary tale, but I've never seen it attributed to anyone in any of the versions forwarded to me. There are some who claim this isn't a fable at all, that it's "based on a true story," but a search of newspaper articles in North Carolina, where this supposedly happened, yielded no stories that come close to resembling this fascinating story. In fact, the police chief in the town where this story supposedly transpired told me he's never heard anything about it.

This tale reads like something that was crafted by a creative writer for a community watchdog group's newsletter, police bulletin, or someone who pens mini-sermons for a non-denominational church.

It also has the ring of one of those TV "after school specials" filled with high drama and a deep message.

In any case, this is one of the most widely disseminated legends on the Internet, presented here in a slightly truncated version. It almost always begins with the header "Something to Think About."

Shannon could hear the footsteps behind her as she walked toward home. The thought of being followed home made her heart beat faster. "You're being silly, no one is following you" she told herself. To be safe, she began to walk faster, but the footsteps kept up with her pace. She was afraid to look back and glad she was almost home. She saw the porch light and ran the rest of the way to her house.

Later she logged on to her computer under her screen name, ByAngel213. Checking her e-mail buddy list, she saw that her friend GoTo123 was online. She sent him an instant message.

ByAngel213: Hi! I'm glad you're on! I thought someone was following me home today. It was really weird!

GoTo123: You watch too much TV. Why would someone be following you? Don't you live in a safe neighborhood?

ByAngel213: Ot course I do. I guess it was just my imagination.

GoTo123: Unless you gave your name out online. You haven't done that, have you?

ByAngel123: Of course not. I'm not stupid you know.

GoTo123: Did you have a softball game after school today?

ByAngel123: Yes and we won!

GoTo123: What is your team called again?

ByAngel123: The Canton Cats. We have tiger paws on our uniforms.

GoTo123: Do you pitch or what?

ByAngel123: No, I play second base. I have to go now anddo my homework before my parents get home.

The individual with the screen name of GoTo123 decided it was time to teach Angel a lesson, one she would never forget. He went to the member menu and began to search for her profile. When it came up, he highlighted it and printed it out. He took out a pen and began to write down what he knew about Angel so far:

Name: Shannon.

Birthday: Jan. 3, 1985. Age: 13.

State where she lived: North Carolina

Hobbies: softball, chorus, skating, going to the mall

He knew she lived in the town of Canton. He knew she stayed by herself until 6:30 every evening. He knew she played softball on Thursday afternoons and the team was named the Canton Cats. In previous online conversations, she had told him her favorite number was 7 and she attended Canton Junior High School. "She doesn't even know what she's done," he thought to himself.

Shannon didn't tell her parents about the incident on the way home from the ballpark that day. She didn't want them to make a scene and stop her from walking home alone from softball games. Parents were always overreacting.

By Thursday, Shannon had forgotten about the footsteps following her the week before. Her game was in full swing when suddenly she felt someone staring at her. It was then that the memory came back.

She glanced up from her second base position to see a man watching her closely. He was leaning against the fence behind first base and smiled when she looked at him. He didn't look scary, so she quickly dismissed the fear she felt.

After the game, he sat in the bleachers while she talked to the coach. She noticed the man's smile once again as she walked past him.

He noticed the name on the back of her shirt. He knew he had found her. Quietly, he walked a safe distance behind her. He didn't want to frighten her and have to explain what he was doing.

It was only a few blocks to Shannon's home, and once he saw where she lived he quickly returned to the park to get his car. Now he had to wait. He decided to get a bite to eat until the time came to go to Shannon's house. He went to a fast food restaurant and sat there until it was time to make his move.

Shannon was in her room later that evening when she heard voices in the living room. Her father called for her. She came downstairs and there was the man from the softball game in her living room.

"Sit down," said her father. "This man is a policeman and he just told me a very interesting story."

"Do you know who I am?" the man asked Shannon.

"No," Shannon answered.

"I am your friend online, GoTo123."

Shannon was stunned. "That's impossible! GoTo is a kid my age! He's 14 and he lives in Michigan!"

The man smiled. "I know I told you all that, but it wasn't true. You see Shannon, there are people online who pretend to be kids; I was one of them. But while others do it to find kids and hurt them, I belong to a group of parents who do it to protect kids from predators. I came here to find you to teach you how dangerous it is to give out too much information to people online. You told me enough about yourself to make it easy for me to find you."

Shannon said, "You don't live in Michigan?"

He laughed. "No, I live in Raleigh. It made you feel safe to think I was so far away, didn't it?"

She nodded.

"I had a friend who had a daughter like you and she had an online friend too," the man said. "Only she wasn't as lucky. The guy found her and murdered her while she was home alone. Kids are taught not to tell anyone when they are alone, yet they do it all the time when they're online. I hope you've learned a lesson from this and you won't do it again."

"I won't," Shannon promised.

"Will you tell others about this so they'll be safe?"

"It's a promise!"

That night Shannon and her mom and dad thanked God for protecting Shannon from a tragic situation.

Please send this to as many people as you can to teach them not to give any information about themselves. This world we live in today is too dangerous to give out even your age, let alone anything else. Be safe! PASS THIS ON!

Kind of like an episode of *Touched by An Angel*, isn't it? However, it might be a more dramatic touch if the cop told Shannon it was *his* little girl who was killed by an online predator.

As for the dad in the story, it would probably be a little more realistic if he punched the cop out for needlessly scaring the crap out of his daughter. In fact, most police forces in the country would probably fire or at least suspend an officer who went online and posed as a 14-year-old boy to stalk a 13-year-old girl in order to teach her a lesson.

Online April Fools' tales

Every year on April Fool's Day, at least a dozen elaborately constructed hoaxes are released on the Internet. In the Stone Age of the 1980s, when we still clung to the belief that cyberspace would be the last and greatest frontier for philosophical debate, lofty thought, and global communication, it was easy to fall for April Fool's Day pranks. Bogus press releases and phony warnings of impending computer doom were taken seriously by many of us in the media, and were often picked up by serious news organizations as legitimate stories. Now it's almost become a sporting event.

There have been literally hundreds of these pranks over the last decade. The ones excerpted here are representative of the genre.

George Lucas abandons *Star Wars Prequels*
April 1, 1997, 8:13 AM EST
By Kevin Somers

(HOLLYWOOD)—With the *Star Wars Trilogy Special Editions* still gobbling up sales receipts at the box office, some bad news has arisen from the Lucasfilm camp.

George Lucas, creator of *Star Wars* and its two sequels, has retracted his promise of a second trilogy of the *Star Wars* films. Mere days ago, Lucasfilm announced plans to start principal photography on *Star Wars—Episode 1* on Sept. 8 of this year. The film was already deep into preproduction. Trouble began late last week when Lucas scrapped 70 percent of the script for the third part of the new trilogy.

When asked why he would turn down the chance to again thrill filmgoers with his sci-fi epic, as well as pass up what would invariably be a windfall in box office grosses, Lucas was quoted as saying "It just isn't going well. Casting has been difficult. We've been unable to find anyone suitable for the roles." Lucas also said that technological limitations have failed to sustain his vision of the films. "I've waited this long for [the technology] to catch up with my imagination, but we're not quite there yet." Lucas plans to return to the project eventually, "but not for a while."

The films were to take place several years before the existing trilogy. The first film of the proposed second trilogy, *Balance of the Force*, was to open in May 1999.

(Reuters/Variety)

I give four stars to this parody story. The byline, the dateline, the parenthetical paraphrasing in the bogus quotes—all nicely done, in the style of a professional journalist. The story has the feel of authenticity, and no doubt launched a million anxiety attacks among dedicated Jedi-heads.

By the time you read this, of course, the fourth *Star Wars* movie has already opened and become one of the top 5 hits of all time.

Bill Gates runs for president

April 1, 1996, 8:20 AM EST

BELLEVUE (CNN)—In a terse press release this morning, Bill Gates announced he would "succeed where Forbes has failed." In other words, he intends to be part of the presidential race—and win it. "I will run as an independent candidate well above out-dated quarrels opposing Democrats and Republicans," he wrote. "I will bring the Information Highway into every American Home. We are entering the era of Digital Democracy," he added.

The press release didn't mention whether he intended to resign from his current position at Microsoft. According to rumors, even though he set his company on a new course to try to tap the vast potential of the Internet, he is secretly doubting this attempt will succeed in the long run, and is now looking for new challenges, and might relinquish his position. Bill Gates could not be reached for comment.

Uploaded 04/01/1996 — 09:17 PST

While the idea of Bill Gates running for president isn't completely preposterous, this attempt to hornswaggle people is pretty weak. Compared to the bogus *Star Wars* story, this is an amateurish attempt to imitate an actual wire service story. You wouldn't put the "succeed where Forbes has failed" quote in your lead, you'd simply say, "In one of the most stunning political announcements in recent history, Microsoft founder Bill Gates has stated his intentions to run for the presidency."

And consider this quote: "I will run as an independent candidate well above out-dated quarrels opposing Democrats and Republicans." Huh? One would like to think Bill Gates actually makes sense when he speaks.

Then there's the factor of timing. By April of 1996, we were already well into the primary season; it would have been a little late for Gates to make a serious run at the presidency.

Some other dubious postings:

- Mattel introduces "Hacker Barbie," the first computer rendition of the pneumatic doll.
- Russia joins the cyberspace race with a with an invitation for everyone to "open a flask of vodka."
- Shamed skater Tonya Harding writes a letter sarcastically "thanking" everyone for their support.
- Microsoft announces its intention to purchase the Vatican.

The wackiness on April 1 knows no bounds.

Also popular on April Fool's Day are the doomsday warnings about mysterious and deadly viruses that will "erase everything from your hard drive" if you even dare to look at the file containing the killer bug. Everything from screen savers featuring the Budweiser frogs to programs from America Online have been identified (falsely of course) as carriers of dangerous viruses. These messages are usually pretty scary because even though your instincts tell you it's not a legitimate warning, you know there are 15-year-old geniuses holed up in their bedrooms somewhere who do have the ability and the warped sense of humor to create havoc on the Internet.

For that reason, I never open a file from an unknown sender, whether it's April Fool's Day or Arbor Day.

The PC cupholder

Time now for a quickie urban legend devoid of any false information or bogus quotes. It's just fun.

A computer neophyte calls a technical help hotline:

Caller: "The cup holder on my PC is broken."

Technical Support Representative (TSR): "The cup holder?"

Caller: "You know, the cup holder attached to the front of the modem."

TSR: "I'm confused. What are we talking about, some kind of freebie you were given with the computer? Is this an attachment you got at a computer trade show?"

Caller: "No, no, no. It's part of the computer. You push a button and it slides right out. The problem is, I slammed my chair into it and it snapped off, and I can't figure out how to reattach it. It's a shame, too, because I really liked having that cup holder there."

(A long silence.)

TSR: "Um, that's not a cup holder, that's the load drawer of your CD-ROM, sir."

Chapter Seven
Tall Tales of the Rich and Famous

I t's amazing how many people profess to know the "in side scoop" about celebrities. Amazingly, these folks who have the inside dirt don't even work in the entertainment industry; heck, most of 'em have never even been to Los Angeles. Nevertheless, they "know" these things to be true.

Why do we all buy into these tales so eagerly? Maybe it's because we're so envious of those blessed few who seem to be living such charmed lives that we can't help but concoct, spread, and swallow such gossip.

I'm naming names in this section not to perpetuate these urban legends, but to shine the light of truth on them as showbiz myths. Not surprisingly, most celebs and their representatives are usually reluctant to even comment on such rumors—you don't want to dignify these stories by even acknowledging they're out there. But they are, and they're not going to fade away naturally...

Richard Gere
and
the gerbil

The Richard Gere gerbil rumor is one of the most enduring and more mean-spirited urban legends of our times. It is so ingrained in the pop consciousness that it seemed only natural the self-referential kids in *Scream* would make a joke about it. Of course, everyone has heard the story by now and nobody believes it's true.

You don't really think Richard Gere was once rushed to a hospital emergency room, where doctors found that a gerbil had become lodged in his rectum during a wild bout of sexual play, do you?

The UL is probably a derivation of a story I heard many times in the 1970s, involving either an anonymous disco dancer, or, in some cases, John Travolta himself, who passes out from excessive partying and is brought to an emergency room where doctors remove his ultra-tight white pants and find that the guy had taped a sausage to his inner thigh. In both stories, the point seems to be that the macho king is not the man he appears to be.

Before Gere was named the "star" of the gerbil story, local television personalities and politicians in cities from New York to Tulsa to Kansas City were the subject of the same story. In dozens of cities, people who claimed to have sources like "a buddy of mine who is married to the best friend of the emergency room nurse," were confidently claiming that the mayor or city councilman or the guy who does the local weather had been in the hospital recently, having a furry little creature extracted from his buttocks.

The tabloid press tried for years to chase down the gerbil story, but nobody was ever able to find the least bit of concrete evidence confirming that Gere (or for that matter, anyone) has ever been "de-gerbilized" by emergency room physicians.

Why was Richard Gere singled out as the target of the gerbil story? Perhaps because his sexuality has been the subject of coarse speculation. Around the time *Pretty Woman* was released, an anonymously circulated fax landed in Hollywood offices and in hundreds of newsrooms. It was supposedly from an animal rights group, protesting Gere's "inhumane treatment" of gerbils—an obvious reference to the rumor that was already fairly well known by then. Nobody ever figured out where that fax originated, but it helped fuel a fire that still burns nearly a decade later.

Gere himself has never commented directly on the rumor, but in 1991, Barbara Walters gently asked Gere about "salacious rumors." Gere stated in typical Zen fashion, "If I am a cow and someone says I'm a zebra it doesn't make me a zebra."

In a Sept. 5, 1995 piece in the *Palm Beach Post*, reporter/editor Mike Walker of the *National Enquirer* was asked about his dogged efforts to confirm the Gere/gerbil story. Walker told the *Post* he'd been trying to nail the story for years but was convinced it was completely without merit.

Mariah Carey's callous remark

A lot of people seem to resent Mariah Carey. They apparently feel she's been just too darn lucky in life, and needs to be put in her place. If only the world knew what an uncaring and self-centered person she really is! For proof of this, you should consider what Carey said in a 1996 interview when she addressed her struggles to stay thin: "When I watch TV and see those poor starving kids all over the world, I can't help but cry. I mean, I'd love to be skinny like that, but not with all those flies and death and stuff."

Can you believe she'd say something like that? Only somebody who's lived a sheltered life filled with adoring fans and untold riches could look at broadcasts of starving children and envy their physiques!

Had Carey issued such a remark, she'd deserve to be flogged for it. However, she's never said anything close to that, and yet the quote has dogged the singing superstar for more than three years. It first appeared in an interview published on the Internet—a parody interview concocted by a prankster writing for the Cupcake web site. Harmless enough, but the quote was picked up by several publications, including the British newspaper *The*

Independent, the San Francisco *Chronicle* and *Ms.* magazine. (By this point the fictitious web site interview had given way to a supposed radio interview Carey had given.)

One Internet scholar/philosopher posted the quote and then launched into a two-page essay about the greater meaning of such a remark. "Statements like Ms. Carey's often make one wonder if human nature is so inescapably flawed that eventually the species will forget how to breathe."

Relax—she never said it.

By the fall of 1996, the quote was being denied by Carey's publicist—Carey herself denied it in a press conference in London—but the line was still floating out there as a legitimate comment, often appearing in those little boxes in newspapers and magazines where they feature notable quotes from celebrities.

Never a favorite with the critics or sophisticated music fans, Carey was an easy target for editors and writers who *wanted* the quote to be real. Who cares if she does charity work and benefit concerts? Why bother to contact her representatives to find out if she really said such a horrendous thing about starving children? Better to run with the quote and let readers howl at the insensitivity of the rich and famous star.

Shortly after the "starving kids" rumor appeared to finally be dying down, Carey was victimized by another bogus quote. After King Hussein of Jordan died in February of 1999, the following post appeared on the Internet:

USA Today, Monday, Feb. 8, 1999

"Mariah Carey was one of the first celebrities to comment on the death of the king of Jordan. Mariah told CNN,

'I'm inconsolable at the present time. I was a very good friend of Jordan, he was probably the greatest basketball player this country has ever seen. We will never see his like again.'

"When told by reporters it was King Hussein of Jordan who had died and not Michael Jordan, Mariah was then led away by security in a state of confusion."

Once again, we're invited to believe the pop star is an out-and-out nincompoop with a first-grader's comprehension of world events. Of course, Carey offered no such quote to CNN, and *USA Today* featured no such item.

Janet Reno's definition of a cult

In an interview on *60 Minutes* in 1994, Janet Reno gave her definition of a "cultist."

"A cultist is one who has a strong belief in the Bible and the Second Coming of Christ," Reno said. "One who frequently attends Bible studies, gives to Christian causes, who home-schools their children, has accumulated survival foods, has a strong belief in the Second Amendment, and who distrusts Big Government. Any of these may qualify a person as a cultist but certainly more than one of these would cause us to look at this person as a threat, and his family as being in a risk situation that qualified for government interference."

By that criteria, there were would be at least 100 million cultists in the United States.

Usually the Reno quote comes attached with warnings from concerned citizens who say things like, "Are you a cultist? According to Janet Reno's definition, you better hope so! Reno feels that any God-fearing citizen who believes in the Constitutional right to bear arms is in fact a danger to the country! Everyone in this country—the so-called "Land of the Free"—should copy this and send it along to family and friends."

Let's remember that the supposed *60 Minutes* interview with Reno occurred in 1994, a year after the siege in Waco. Even though Koresh and the adults who holed up in that compound must also bear the responsibility for the tragedy, Reno's actions made the Branch Davidian cult into heroes in the eyes of many conservatives who believed the attorney general's tactics seriously threatened their freedoms. They *wanted* to believe her definition of a cultist extended far beyond Waco.

In some versions of the *60 Minutes* quote, Reno addresses the Branch Davidian tragedy by name. After listing the traits that would attract the interest, and arouse the suspicions of, the government, Reno explained, "Waco was one of those situations that qualified under our definition of people being at risk that necessitates government action to save them."

Chilling words—but words never spoken by Reno. In the spring of 1995, when the rumor reached the desks of a couple of congressmen who made inquiries about its validity, the Justice Department issued a statement that read, in part, "The plain fact is that the quote is a hoax. The Attorney General has never been interviewed on *60 Minutes*. She has never discussed cults, or tried to define one. There is nothing in the counterfeit quote that guides government policy. The quote first appeared...in the August 1993 'Paul Revere Newsletter' of the Christian Defense League in Flora, Illinois. The information came by telephone from a woman in Florida whose name was not noted. The newsletter subsequently ran a retraction."

The controversy died down for a couple of years, but resurfaced again in 1998—only this time Reno was said to have made the comments at a banquet for the Bureau of Alcohol, Firearms and Tobacco.

I've yet to uncover a scintilla of evidence that Janet Reno has even had dreams about defining a cultist.

The misunderstanding on the elevator

For more than 20 years, a black celebrity has been getting on an elevator and uttering a command that is misinterpreted by a frightened white woman, who always reacts to the command in the same way.

First the celebrity was Bill Cosby, then it was Richard Pryor, then Lionel Ritchie. Sports figures such as Mike Tyson, Magic Johnson, Wilt Chamberlain, Dennis Rodman, O.J. Simpson, Mean Joe Greene and Shaquille O'Neal have also been on the elevator. In later versions it was Eddie Murphy, and in 1999 I heard it was Sean "Puffy" Combs.

Sometimes the elevator misunderstanding takes place in New York; other times it's Las Vegas. But while the celebrity and the locale change from telling to telling, the story remains essentially the same.

Two middle-aged white women from the Midwest come to New York for a business convention. They're in the elevator of a hotel in Manhattan, heading down to the lobby, when it stops on the 12th floor and an entourage enters consisting of three very intimidating-looking black men dressed in leather and gold chains, and a growling Doberman who bares its teeth at the women.

"Sit!" commands one of the men—and the women immediately obey, sitting on the floor of the elevator.

"No, I meant the dog!" says the man, who apologizes to the women and helps them to their feet, as his companions try to stifle their laughter. The women nervously laugh off the incident and explain to the man that they've never been to New York before. In an effort to downplay the incident, they make idle, awkward conversation. The women also ask the celebrity if he can recommend a good restaurant. He does just that, and the two groups part company in the lobby.

Later that evening, the two women have a lovely meal at the restaurant recommended by the man from the elevator. When they ask the waiter for the check, he explains that it's already been taken care of, courtesy of Eddie Murphy, the famous comedian and actor.

One of the woman says, "But why would Eddie Murphy pay for our dinner? We don't know him, and he certainly doesn't know us."

And then it dawns on her. Murphy was the man on the elevator, the one who issued the command to "Sit." Still feeling bad about the misunderstanding, he had arranged to pick up the check.

In another variation, the incident takes place in Las Vegas and a white woman is so flustered by the "Sit!" confusion that when the elevator doors open, she dashes out of the elevator and doesn't even realize she has dropped her gambling chips or bucket of coins. The next morning, room service brings her the winnings, plus a $100 chip and a note from the celebrity, thanking her for the best laugh he's had in a long time and wishing her good luck at the tables.

In the early 1980s, when I first heard the story, baseball great Reggie Jackson was supposedly the guy on the elevator, and columnists at a number of newspapers (including the *Cincinnati Enquirer* and the *Detroit Free Press*) were reporting the incident as fact—or at least something they believed could be true, based on their reliable sources. Jackson and his agent issued a number of denials, but it did little to stop the story from spreading.

UL FOOTNOTE. It's possible this UL has its origins in an episode of the old *Bob Newhart Show*, the one in which Newhart played a psychiatrist, as the source for this story. In the episode, one of Bob's patients is a large black man with a black Great Dane named Whitey; after his session with Dr. Hartley, the black man goes into the lobby, where Jerry the dentist is hanging out. The man says, "Sit, Whitey!"—whereupon Jerry perches on Carol the receptionist's desk.

Elvis
Presley's
Harley

A young man from New Zealand, fresh out of college, decides to spend a few months in the United
States, visiting as many tourist attractions as possible, from the Statue of Liberty to Disney World to
Graceland to the Grand Canyon. While hitchhiking in
Arizona, he wanders into a small town with not much
more than a gas station, a tavern, and a couple of stores.
The young man slips into the tavern to take a break from
the heat and winds up playing pool with a local character, a burned-out, aging hippie who is kind of a local
legend.

After several games of pool and bottles of beer, the
old hippie says to the young traveler, "You know, you
remind me a lot of myself back when I was your age.
When I got out of school I went to Europe and back-
packed for three months before I ran out of money. Then
I came back here and hitchhiked all the way across
America. It was the best time of my life.

"But you know what? Times have changed, brother.
It's a crazy world out there, and it just ain't safe to be
hitchhiking any more. That's why I'm going to sell you my
motorcycle."

Urban Legends

The New Zealander figures there's some sort of scam in the works. "That's an interesting offer," he says, "but I'm really not looking to buy a motorcycle. I don't have that much money."

"Ah, that's all right, I'll give you a good price," says the old hippie. "The way I figure it, my traveling days are over. I ain't got no kids of my own, and I'd hate to see this Harley of mine go to waste. Tell you what, I'll *give* it to you, if you promise to take good care of it."

Now the young kid is sure something is amiss, but he agrees to take a look at the bike, which he's sure is going to be some broken-down old thing in need of dire repair.

But it's not. It's a slightly beat-up but still working red-and-white 1956 KH. The New Zealand traveler doesn't want to take advantage of the old hippie, so he offers to pay him $1,000, which represents the total amount of his savings. The hippie reluctantly accepts the check, and the kid is on his way. A few weeks later, he stops in Michigan, decides he'll apply for permanent resident status, and look for work there.

Fast forward five years. Our friend from New Zealand gets laid off from his job, and he's short on cash, so he places a classified ad offering the motorcycle for sale. One of the first prospective buyers gets very excited as he inspects the bike, and he offers to give the guy a check for $40,000 on the spot. The kid gets suspicious and tells the prospective buyer he'll have to get back to him.

His next move is to visit a local Harley-Davidson dealer to get the motorcycle appraised. After waiting around for a few minutes, the guy is asked to join the appraiser in the manager's office, and he's soon offered $100,000 for the bike, no questions asked.

"What is it about this motorcycle?" says the guy, but he gets no answers. When he gets home, he calls the toll-free number of Harley-Davidson and is put in touch with an expert who asks him to describe the bike. Suddenly the expert interrupts him and says, "I'm authorized to offer you a half-million dollars for that motorcycle, son."

"Deal!" says our guy.

The next day, a representative from Harley-Davidson shows up with the necessary paperwork, and the transaction is completed. Clutching the cashier's check for $500,000, the guy says, "Now will you tell me what's up with this bike?"

"Sure," says the Harley-Davidson rep. "Remove the gas cap and take a look at the inscription on it?"

The guy does just that, and for the first time he sees an engraving that's been there all along: "To James Dean, Love, Elvis."

"Some guy paid $3 million for Mark McGwire's home run ball, so you can only imagine what a one-of-a-kind piece of memorabilia like this would be worth," says the Harley rep. "Heck, you probably could have gotten $5 million!"

If there was any friendship between Elvis Presley and James Dean, it would have been short-lived, as the King was just coming into prominence when Dean was killed in his Porsche Spyder on Sept. 5, 1955.

Todd Morgan, the creative director at Graceland, told me he first started hearing the rumors in 1994. "This became a mild source of aggravation and amusement, because these claims were totally bogus from start to finish," he said.

The version Morgan hears most often is that Graceland has three of the four Harleys owned by Elvis, and has a standing offer of $1 million for the fourth. None of this is true.

Harley Davidson historian Dr. Martin Jack Rosenblum told me that the version he hears most often is about a guy who is riding across the country on his motorcycle, when it breaks down near a farm somewhere in Wisconsin. A farmer shows the guy his own motorcycle, which has a plate under the seat that says, "To James Dean, from Elvis Presley." He buys the motorcycle from the farmer, and a bidding war ensues between Jay Leno and the Harley Davidson company, with Leno eventually purchasing the rare piece for $1 million. (In a 1999 radio appearance in Nashville, Leno was asked about the story and said it was complete nonsense.)

Rosenblum told me thinks the rumor got started in 1993, when he purchased a Harley that once belonged to Elvis. "Presley bought the bike in 1956 from his local dealer, but no plaque or plate was ever made. Harley Davidson never makes special plates or engraves special messages on its bikes."

Presley gave the bike to a friend—not James Dean—and Rosenblum bought it from the friend. End of story.

Tiger Woods
at the
strip club

When Tiger Woods roared onto the scene a few years ago, the hype was overwhelming. After Woods was named *Sports Illustrated's* "Sportsman of the Year" in 1996 and won the Masters in 1997, the expectations were raised to the level of the absurdly unrealistic. He was featured in a series of Nike ads, was mobbed by crowds who treated him like a rock star, and appeared on the covers of magazines, from *GQ* to *SI* as frequently as Michael Jordan.

Tiger's fame was such that he was accorded perhaps the ultimate celebrity status symbol in late 1996 and early 1997—his very own urban legend, told to this day as a true anecdote on sports talk shows and in barroom conversation.

Here's how it was told to me. In 1996, when Woods was just 20, in Las Vegas for a tournament, he and a group of friends decided to check out one of the infamous strip joints in town. All of Tiger's buddies were waved in, but the surly bouncer put a meaty paw on the young golfer's chest, regarded Tiger's youthful visage, and demanded identification. Tiger figured that his celebrity status would gain him immediate entrance, so he confidently took out his driver's license and handed it to the bouncer, who shined a flashlight on it and frowned.

"Says here you're only 20, Mr. Woods," he said. "Sorry pal, you've got to be 21 to see what goes on in here."

"But I'm the Tiger!" exclaimed the golfing superstar.

"Hey, I don't care if you're the lion or the bear, you're not getting in," the bouncer replied.

The Oct. 28 sports section of the *Chicago Tribune* referred to a "Milwaukee paper's" report about Woods playing in the Quad-City Classic tournament and trying to get into an area bar, only to be thwarted by a bouncer who carded him.

"Woods: 'I don't need an ID. I'm the Tiger.'

"Bouncer: 'I don't care if you're the Lion King. You ain't getting in here unless you have an ID.' "

What are the odds that two bouncers in two different locales would use similar lines to turn back such a beloved celebrity?

I dug up that "Milwaukee paper" account, which the *Tribune* had quoted accurately. It originally appeared in a sports notebook column in the Oct. 20, 1996 edition of the *Milwaukee Journal Sentinel*, with the caveat that the incident was "said to have taken place at the American Bar, a popular joint in the Quad Cities area."

Let's get real here. Even when Woods was 20, he would have had no trouble gaining entrance into any club or bar in the world. What tavern owner or strip club operator wouldn't love to have a picture on his wall of Tiger Woods whooping it up in his joint?

Tommy Hilfiger unfairly maligned

Just this year, a colleague of mine (who is black) told me she would never let her two sons wear anything designed by Tommy Hilfiger, "because of what he said on Oprah's show." Her strong but misguided stance proves once again that urban legends die hard.

A typical version of the story:

"Did you see designer Tommy Hilfiger's recent appearance on the *Oprah Winfrey Show*? He said that if he had known so many blacks and Chinamen were going to buy his clothes, he wouldn't have made them so nice. 'I wish those people would not buy my clothes,' he told Oprah. 'They were made for upper-class whites.' To her credit, Oprah threw him off the show and advised her viewers to burn any Tommy Hilfiger clothes they might have in their possession. She also suggested that everyone boycott Tommy Hilfiger. What a great idea. That'll teach him a lesson about his racist ways."

The facts:

Hilfiger is so popular with black rappers that he has been immortalized in hip-hop songs.

A large percentage of Hilfiger's customers happen to be minorities.

The chairman of Hilfiger's company happens to be Asian-American.

Hilfiger told the *Los Angeles Times*, in 1996, "I'm complimented [that many rappers wear my clothes]. I know they can wear anything, yet they choose my clothes. It is a true, true honor. I think these kids are so cool."

Hilfiger never made the cavalierly racist remarks. In fact, he's never even been a guest on *Oprah* Nevertheless, the remark was getting so much play on the rumor circuit that the company issued an official denial:

"Tommy Hilfiger did not make the alleged inappropriate racial comments...Hilfiger wants his clothing to be enjoyed by people of all backgrounds and his collections are put together with the broadest cross-section of individuals in mind. To reinforce this, he features models of all ethnic backgrounds on his fashion shows and advertisements."

On January 11, 1999, Winfrey took the extraordinary step of addressing the UL at the beginning of her program.

"I just wanted to set the record straight once and for all," she said. "The rumor claims that clothing designer Tommy Hilfiger came on this show and made racist remarks, and that I kicked him out. I want to say this is not true because it just never happened. Tommy Hilfiger has never appeared on this show. Read my lips: Tommy Hilfiger has never appeared on this show! And all of the people who claim they saw or heard it. It never happened. I've never even met Tommy Hilfiger."

Unfortunately, even a straightforward denial like that will never totally kill the rumor. To this day there are people who *swear* they saw the show in which Oprah kicked Hilfiger off the stage.

Hilfiger has been dogged by that rumor for two or three years—but Liz Claiborne has been fighting a similar rumor for the better part of an entire decade. (In fact the Hilfiger legend is probably a spinoff of the Claiborne myth.) First, Claiborne was accused of uttering racist remarks to CNN's fashion reporter Elsa Klensch; then it was reported that she was a guest on *Oprah* when she made the unforgivable comments.

"Don't buy Liz Claiborne clothes!" begins one fax I received a couple of years ago. "Liz Claiborne is a racist, and she showed her true nature on a recent episode of the *Oprah Winfrey Show*. Oprah wore a Liz Claiborne gown and had Claiborne on as a favor to promote Claiborne's clothing, but Claiborne turned on her during the broadcast when she said, 'My clothes were not designed for black women.'

"When Oprah asked her what she meant by that, Claiborne elaborated: 'My clothes are not designed for black women, Oprah, because black women's hips are too big and they look horrible in my clothes.' A gasp went through the crowd, but everyone cheered when Oprah threw Claiborne off the set. When they came back from the commercial, Oprah was in a bathrobe, and with tears in her eyes she urged everyone to boycott Claiborne, who had told Oprah during the break that she supported the KKK!"

You'll recall the *Oprah Winfrey Show* was also mentioned as the program on which a psychic predicted a massacre on a college campus. Before Oprah took over as the queen of daytime television, *Donahue* was often cited as the show on which some remarkable incident or comment took place. To source a specific program, especially one with such credibility as Oprah's, is no accident; it gives the rumor a certain veracity that it wouldn't have if, say, *Springer* was mentioned. Hearing that it happened on *Oprah* means it must be true. For years, publicists for Oprah's program have patiently told reporters and irate fans not to worry—none of these alleged incidents ever occurred.

In 1997, a new bastardization of the rumor surfaced. This time it was the popular hip-hop singer Lauryn Hill who had appeared on *Oprah* or some other show, stunning the audience of mostly middle-aged, suburban housewives by declaring, "I'd rather kill my baby than have white people listening to my music." A caller to Howard Stern's show claimed he'd heard her make the remarks on MTV. Not true.

Keanu Reeves marries David Geffen

Rumors about a wedding between actor Keanu Reeves and media mogul David Geffen crested in late 1995 and early 1996, as media circles swirled with off-the-record but increasingly loud whispers about a ceremony in Malibu or Mexico, with Geffen and Reeves exchanging vows in front of a small gathering of their closest friends. Afterward Geffen supposedly took Reeves on a "honeymoon shopping spree" at noted clothier Barney's, where the actor ran up thousands of dollars in charges. Reeves has been linked with many women, but he played a bisexual hustler in *My Own Private Idaho*, which unfortunately provides enough fodder for the rumor mill to start churning.

Geffen reacted to the wedding story with good humor. He also opined that the rumor most likely wasn't started by gays looking to make Reeves one of their own (for lack of a better term), but by someone wishing to hurt Reeves—perhaps even a woman looking to get even with him.

"I think these stories reflect frustration on the part of some women who simply do not get the response they want from these men," Geffen told *Vanity Fair*. "It could be that the men are not interested, or they may be involved with someone else, but it's easier to label them as gay."

The truth was that at the time the rumor was in heavy rotation on the urban legend play list, Geffen hadn't even met Reeves, let alone embarked on a whirlwind romance culminating in an oceanside marriage ceremony.

In a 1995 profile, *Out* magazine was the first publication to directly question Reeves about the supposed wedding, and he of course denied it (while also saying, "That's cool, that's cool," when told many gay men find him attractive). "Oh, yes!" he told the magazine when asked about the rumors. "I first heard it when I was in Winnepeg, on my answering machine. My friend Claire called and said, 'Hey, I heard that you went and got married, congratulations.'

"I guess I should return the clothes," Reeves said jokingly. But he added: "I didn't really think about [the rumor] much."

Reeves also told *Vanity Fair* the story wasn't true, but he refused to state his sexual orientation for the record: "There's nothing wrong with being gay," he said, "so to deny it is to make a judgment. And why make a big deal out of it?"

Paul Newman's ice cream cone

Even the most jaded types find themselves acting differently when in the presence of a celebrity. If you're in a restaurant or at a ballgame and a famous person happens to be seated nearby, you can try all you want to be cool and blasé about the whole thing, but you're very aware that you're doing it.

Many people don't even try to play it cool when they see a celebrity, even if it's someone whose work they don't particularly appreciate. I've seen perfectly rational, mature adults turn into raving idiots just because a mid-level rock star or an actor from a popular sitcom has entered a room. In my adventures as an entertainment journalist, I saw the crazed look in people's eyes when they realized they were coming face to face with a major celebrity.

This is not to say I think I'm above such silly but usually harmless starstruck behavior. I was a jaded, 30-year-old reporter who had met hundreds of celebrities when I was introduced to Paul Newman, and I managed to maintain an outward appearance of calm as I said, "How ya doin' Paul, I'm Richard Roeper from Chicago," but inside there was a little man running through the corridors of my brain, hollering, "We're meeting Cool Hand Luke, Butch Cassidy and Fast Eddie Felson! Yeah!"

Imagine being Paul Newman and knowing that every time you meet someone, they're thinking something like that. It must be extremely flattering and extremely exhausting. Paul Newman never gets a day off from being Paul Newman—not even when he's waiting in line at an ice cream shop on Main Street in a little town called Urban Legendville, USA.

Actually the shop was located in Massachusetts, or in the Hamptons, or in Connecticut, as the story goes. A crabby old gal was in line at the town's quaint ice cream shop, muttering under her breath about the slow service. "These kids today are so lazy," she said. "Lazy and just plain stupid!"

"Ah, they're not so bad," says a gravelly voice behind her.

She turned to give the man a piece of her mind—and that's when she found herself looking right into the famous blue eyes of Paul Newman, her all-time favorite movie star! For one of the few times in her life, the woman was reduced to a babbling, nearly incoherent fool as she prattled on to the smiling Newman about everything and anything.

She was still in a daze as she paid for her ice cream cone and walked to her car, shaking with excitement from the experience.

Only when she put the key in the ignition did the woman come to the realization that she didn't have her ice cream cone. She exited the car, hurried back into the shop, marched past everyone who was waiting in line, and berated the young cashier for his stupidity and dishonesty.

The startled cashier said, "But I gave you—"

"Don't interrupt me!" said the lady. "That's the trouble with you young people, you're always interrupting your elders and—"

The woman was interrupted again, this time by a tap on her shoulder. She wheeled around with fire in her eyes, but her anger subsided when she saw that it was none other than Mr. Newman, who had been trying to enjoy his caramel sundae as she began her tirade.

"Don't take it out on the boy," Newman said. "He gave you the ice cream cone, dear. You put it in your pocketbook."

This story was all the rage in the mid-1980s. Usually Paul Newman was the celebrity, but in other instances it was Tom Brokaw, Dan Rather, Robert Redford, or Jack Nicholson.

None of them has ever experienced anything like the ice cream cone incident in real life, though Nicholson once did tell his limo driver to make a diversion to a liquor store on the way to JFK Airport, and he ended up drinking out of a bottle with some of the regulars outside the store, which I think is even funnier than the ice cream cone UL.

Pia Zadora heckled

In recent years, the Golden Globes have managed to attain an aura of credibility, but that was only after a long exile from mainstream attention, during which the awards weren't even telecast. This freeze-out can be attributed largely to the fiasco of 1981, when Pia Zadora, star of *Butterfly*, won a Golden Globe as "Best New Star of the Year," much to the astonishment of anyone who had ever seen her act.

The common belief was that Zadora won due to the influence of her much older producer husband, the extremely wealthy Meshulam Riklis. (When you have fewer than 100 people voting for one of five nominees, it doesn't take that much to sway an election. One can take home a statue with little more than 20 votes.)

Even as Zadora was polishing her Golden Globe, she was the subject of unrelenting humor, especially in Johnny Carson's monologues. As an attractive woman with an unusual name and a ton of chutzpah, Zadora was an easy target.

No wonder she found herself headlining in an urban legend that was really nothing more than an old joke. According to a story that still circulates to this day,

Zadora's husband financed a Broadway production of *The Diary of Anne Frank*. The actress was horribly miscast as a young Jewish girl hiding from the Nazis, and the opening night crowd was barely able to contain its titters as she flung herself about the stage, drifting in and out of her accent and constantly flubbing her lines.

When the Nazis arrived at her house, a jokester in the crowd couldn't resist. He stood up and said in a loud, clear voice: "She's in the attic!" Normally such boorish behavior would be met with harsh retorts, but in this case the crowd actually cheered the heckler, who walked out in triumph.

It almost sounds believable, but it never happened. Zadora has never played the role of Anne Frank, on Broadway or anywhere else.

As Zadora's name faded, I've heard the same story told about Vanna White and former Playboy Playmates Jenny McCarthy and Pamela Anderson. Needless to say, none of these blonde bombshells has ever been cast in a play about a 12-year-old Jewish girl who keeps a written record of her attempt to hide from the Nazis.

Barbra Streisand's porno film

Rumors about big stars who made pornographic movies before they became famous have been around nearly as long as the movie industry itself.

When Joan Crawford was making a name for herself in the mid-1930s, there were rumbles about a stag film in her past. According to some Hollywood historians, MGM honcho Louis B. Mayer even obtained a print, but wasn't convinced it was Crawford in the movie. Marilyn Monroe has also been mentioned as someone who did some sleazy film work before she ever got to Hollywood. I've seen a much-copied, rather blurry video purporting to show young Marilyn posing nude and rolling around for the camera. The film really isn't much more revealing than the photo shoots Marilyn participated in after she became a star.

Barbra Streisand, on the other hand, would absolutely be mortified if the world were to find out she did a hardcore porno film as a young woman. Many believe there is just such a film. This movie has been duped thousands of times and has been passed around for years on the underground circuit, always advertised as "Barbra Streisand's porno movie." There's no sound or dialogue, and the soundtrack is a cheesy, electronic type of thing, obviously added to the movie years after it was made. The black-and-white film appears to have been shot with a single camera, with a few jumps that indicate some editing was involved. For the duration of the film, we see nothing but a young couple on a sofa, engaging in sexual intercourse.

Is the girl in the movie Streisand? Well, if you were to show the movie to a friend and say, "Which Hollywood star does that woman look like?", the only possible answer would be, "Barbra Streisand." There are moments when she smiles and you're almost convinced it's really Streisand.

However, if you concentrate on her face, you begin to realize this is definitely *not* Barbra Streisand. The likely explanation is that somebody somewhere was looking at this old porno movie and noticed the resemblance to Streisand, and started circulating copies to friends, who told their friends, who told their friends, and so on. Some copies have been creatively edited to include still photos of a young Streisand so you can compare her to the porno gal—but this only serves to illustrate the differences between the two women.

Besides, if Streisand really had made such a film, there wouldn't have been that much lag time between the making of the movie and the making of Barbra Streisand, Superstar. Surely the guy who slept with the Streisand lookalike in the film, or the guy who worked the camera, or the citizens who financed the movie would have stepped forward a long time ago and said, "I know that girl!"

It never happened. Why? Because that ain't Streisand in that movie.

Marilyn Manson's *Wonder Years*

Remember Kevin Arnold's best friend on *The Wonder Years*, Paul Pfeiffer? The kid with the big glasses and the prominent nose? Well, the geeky kid grew up to be...shock rocker Marilyn Manson! There's even an Internet site showing Paul's face morphing into Manson's.

Every high schooler in America has heard this one by now. It's the late 1990s version of the old "Eddie Haskell is Alice Cooper" legend that circulated a generation ago.

We seem to like to de-fang our scary rock stars. With his hateful posturing, simulated acts of violence onstage, his creepy androgynous looks, and head-pounding music, Marilyn Manson is a rather intimidating figure for some folks to ponder. But if it turns out he's just the grown-up version of that nice Paul Pfeiffer kid from *The Wonder Years*, now we know he's just acting, don't we?

Alas, Paul is not Marilyn, and Marilyn is not Paul. The character of Paul Pfeiffer was played by actor Josh Saviano, while Marilyn Manson was born Brian Warner in Canton, Ohio, home of the Pro Football Hall of Fame.

In a *Nick at Nite* online chat session with Saviano and fans in 1996, the very first question dealt with the Marilyn Manson story.

Q: "OK, so Josh, there is this huge rumor going around that you are Marilyn Manson. I know this isn't true, but how do you think this rumor got started and are you aware of it?"

SAVIANO: "Yes, I am very much aware of it. I receive close to 20 E-mails a week asking me if this is true. Obviously it's not, but I enjoy the creativity of some people."

Fred Savage, who played Kevin Arnold on *The Wonder Years*, has also heard the rumor umpteen times. He was asked about it on E! Online.

Q: "What did you think about the rumor that Marilyn Manson was Paul from 'The Wonder Years' "?

SAVAGE: "More people have come up and asked me if Paul is Marilyn Manson lately than any other question. The answer is no! I'm getting a little tired of that one."

Manson's calculatedly outrageous behavior has led to several other budding urban legends: while on LSD, he lost an eye after sticking a fork in it; he throws puppies and baby ducks into the crowd at concerts and urges that the cute little animals be killed; he has raped girls on stage; he's getting breast implants; he plans to kill himself in the year 2002 with a knife shaped like a crucifix...

And they say it's only rock 'n' roll...

Julia Child drops a duck

Dan Aykroyd's imitation of Julia Child on *Saturday Night Live* was a classic. Dressed in drag, speaking in a wacky falsetto and making a mess of things in the kitchen, "Child" was unfazed by any mishaps, including the severe injuries she sustained.

Maybe it's the Aykroyd impersonation that convinced us something crazy happened in Julia Child's kitchen way back when, something that fueled the *SNL* bit.

Some of the stories that abound are certainly amusing enough, such as when Child would occasionally take a swig from a bottle of wine or cooking sherry on the air, telling viewers, "Everything tastes better if you have a little nip now and then."

She also supposedly dropped a duck on the kitchen floor, but picked it up, brushed it off, and plunked it right back in the oven. "Who's going to know?" she told viewers. "What are you going to do, throw away a perfectly good bird because you dropped it?"

In a 1995 interview with the *Chicago Tribune*, Child was asked about these rumors. "I never did [drop a duck]. People say, 'But I saw you do that.' Once, while I was flipping a potato pancake, it flipped onto the stove and

I picked it up and put it back in the pan and said, 'You're alone in the kitchen.'

"It's interesting when people say, 'I saw you do it.' Or that 'I saw you pick up the bottle of wine and take a swig of it,' which I would never do."

Child said there was an incident involving a "turkey or something and it was wrapped on a counter in back of me, and it began sliding into the sink," but the turkey didn't hit the floor.

Once again, we have to remember that Julia Child's program was not live—if it were, we'd have to sit in front of the TV for hours, waiting for a goose, or turkey, or a rack of lamb to be cooked. If a turkey ever did hit the floor, or if Ms. Child had felt the urge to take a hit from a bottle of wine, they could have stopped taping and simply done another take.

Celebrity shorts

Here's a quick look at some celebrity urban legends involving embarrassing incidents, secret pasts, and dubious claims. Each of these stories has been in circulation for at least a couple of years, and some have been reported as factual items in gossip columns and feature stories, but I did not uncover a single piece of evidence to lend credence to any of them.

Fred Grandy in Congress

When Fred Grandy, who played Gopher on *The Love Boat*, was elected to the United States House of Representatives, he had a predictably difficult time gaining the respect of the cynical, jaded types on Capitol Hill. Everyone was snickering about "Congressman Gopher"—even though Grandy was a dedicated, intelligent, well-informed fellow.

On the day Grandy was sworn in, he entered an elevator already crowded with a number of congressmen and senators. He could see the knowing glances and the smirking smiles starting to form on some faces; he knew they were thinking, "Hey look, it's Gopher!"

As the elevator doors closed, the congressional page who was operating the elevator turned to Grandy and said, "Lido Deck, sir?"

Everyone burst into laughter, but Grandy didn't think it was funny. He grabbed the page's credentials and ID and had the young man fired. From that point on, people realized it wasn't a good idea to joke with Fred Grandy about his television past.

Unlikely snipers

At least two celebrities with benign images have been "outed" as being former sharpshooters. The grandfatherly Dave Thomas of the Wendy's hamburger chain was alleged to have been in the National Guard, and was one of the troops deployed to Kent State University on May 4, 1970—the day four students were gunned down by National Guardsmen. Thomas supposedly was the one who fired the first shot, a decision that haunts him to this very day and keeps Wendy's PR people awake at night, wondering when some enterprising journalist is going to uncover the story.

Another former military man was the late John Henry Deutchendorff, better known to his millions of fans as John Denver. In the late 1960s, Denver was stationed in Vietnam as a highly trained sniper, and his technique was so legendary it was called "The Denver Method." Denver would hide out in a tree with the sun in a certain position behind him, wait for his prey to come into range; and make a low whistling noise to get their attention. When they'd look up, they'd be momentarily blinded by the sun, and Denver would open fire. Using this method, he killed dozens of Vietcong and was decorated with a ton of medals.

Only after returning to the States and raising his consciousness did Denver feel haunted by what he'd done in Vietnam. He threw away his medals, tore up his commendations, took up the guitar, and embraced a passive lifestyle—but he couldn't totally lose the memories of his years as a sniper. In fact, one of Denver's biggest feel-good hits was a tacit admission of his dark past. "Sunshine on My Shoulders" might have sounded like a sappy little ballad, but in reality, Denver was confronting his 'Nam alter ego, the sniper who waited in the trees for the sunlight to blind his enemies so he could extinguish their lives: "Sunshine on my shoulders, makes me happy..."

Only problem is, John Denver never served in Vietnam. In the 1960s he was already pursuing a musical career.

Epilogue

Y ou're not going to believe what happened to me when I finished this book. I decided to celebrate the completion of the job, so I went to the fridge to see if there was anything cold and refreshing available. I had a six-pack of Miller Genuine Draft chilling—and the best thing about it was, it didn't cost me a nickel. See, to celebrate the millennium, Miller's been giving away coupons good for a free six-pack of any of their fine beer products.[1] All you have to do is respond to the e-mail message that's been making the rounds. It's easy!

As I sipped my free beer, I clicked on the TV and started channel-surfing. An old episode of *Leave it to Beaver* was on. That used to be one of my favorite shows, but now it's just too depressing to watch, knowing that the Beaver died in Vietnam and Eddie Haskell became a porn star who died of AIDS.[2,3]

I clicked over to a showing of *Goldfinger* on cable, but that was upsetting, too. That poor woman covered in gold paint suffocated to death[4], and no one knew it as they were filming the scene! What a tragedy.

I clicked to another station, and there was the actress Jamie Lee Curtis on a talk show. Looking at her in that tight outfit, you'd never guess in a million years that she was born a hermaphrodite.[5]

Just then the phone rang. It was my friend Bob, asking me if I'd checked my e-mail messages in the last hour. When I told him I hadn't, Bob said, "Well, make sure you do before you go to bed tonight. There's a sick little girl named Jessica Mydek who needs our help,[6] and I also included that secret recipe for Mrs. Field's Cookies I was telling you about.[7] Plus, I finally found Kurt Vonnegut's great commencement speech from a few years ago,[8] I think you'll find some valuable life lessons in there."

"Can't wait to access all that valuable information," I told my friend. "So what did you do tonight?"

"I rented a video, but I got more than I bargained for," he told me. "When I popped the tape in my VCR, all of a sudden there's this couple just going at it like crazy. I guess when they returned the video to the store, they left the movie at home and put one of their amateur sex tapes in the box instead![9]"

"The strangest things happen to you," I said. "Like when you tried to buy that 'hot' VCR, and you came home and found out the box had nothing but bricks in it."[10]

"You're telling me. Oh man, look at the time, I've got to go. I've got a date with a nurse who was working in the emergency room the night they brought Travolta in with that sausage taped to his leg."[11]

"You're one lucky guy," I said. "Good night."

I hung up the phone, just as my girlfriend Marisa Tomei[12] walked in.

"I've made a decision," she said. "I'm giving back the Oscar."[13]

Epilogue

If you believed any of the above—especially the part about Marisa Tomei being my girlfriend—you must have decided to read this book from back to front. Any amateur urban legendologist could spot a dozen UL's in the preceding story.

Which brings us to the sequel. The 100 or so too-good-to-be-true tales dissected in this book represent only a small portion of the stories currently in circulation. With your help, I plan on compiling a new collection of UL's for the new millennium. Please feel free to contact me with your favorite urban legends—the fresher the better. No hook-in-the-car-door stories, please.

The "X-Files" has it wrong; the truth *isn't* out there. It's my mission to see that this changes.

Richard Roeper
May, 1999

Write me c/o: The Chicago Sun-Times
401 N. Wabash, Chicago, IL 60611
Fax: 312-321-2120
E-mail: rroeper@suntimes.com

---

[1]Urban legend.
[2,3]Urban legend, urban legend.
[4]UL.
[5]Another UL.
[6]An urban legend.
[7] Ibid.
[8]Ibid, ibid, ibid.
[9]You know it, you love it, you can't live without it: Another urban legend.
[10]UL.
[11]Yep. Urban legend.
[12]Folks, this ain't an urban legend. It's a pathetic male fantasy.
[13]UL.

Notes

The Classics
"They're stealing our kidneys!"
New Orleans Police Dept. notice. Reprinted with permission.
Dog swallows cell phone
Story reprinted with permission from the *London Sun*.
The truth about Furbys
Interview, Tiger Electronics, March 1999.
"A Toy Story of Hairy Espionage; NSA Bans Furby From Spy Agency's Premises," by Vernon Loeb, Pg. A21, *Washington Post*, January 13, 1999
Prehistoric Barbie
Interview with Randall Kremer, public affairs director, Smithsonian Institution, March 1999.
Gang initiation rites
"Better Shop Around For Well-Policed Malls," from "Dear Abby" column, Pg. 17, *Chicago Tribune*, April 23, 1992.
Tainted needles
"Urban Myth Is Reality," by Michael Sluss, Pg B3, *The Roanoke Times*, February. 11, 1999.
"Third Needle Incident is Reported in Pulaski," by Michael Sluss, Pg. 2, *The Roanoke Times*, February 12, 1999.
The Gerber rebate
Statement from Gerber Co. Reprinted with permission.
Craig Shergold's dying wish
Interview with Michelle Lewis, Public Relations Executive with Make-A-Wish Foundation, March 1999.
"Are You Gay?"
Information from USAir obtained from author interview with USAir director of public relations David Castlevetter, March 1999.

Urban Legends

Earthquake squashes car thief

Interview with Judy Canter, Head Librarian for *San Francisco Chronicle*, March 1999.

Interview with San Francisco Public Information Officer Jim Diegman, March 1999.

"Good Luck, Mr. Gorsky"

Interview with NASA's Director of Media Services Brian Welch, April 1999.

NASA transcripts. Reprinted with permission.

The toothbrush bandits

Infinite Jest, by David Foster Wallace, Little Brown and Company, Pg. 55, February 1996.

Legends of Rolling Rock

"Rolling Rock: A 12-Ouncer Takes an Incredible Journey," by Rege Behe, *Pittsburgh Tribune-Review*, Aug. 31, 1997.

"Welcome to the world of AIDS"

Interview with CDC's HIV Media Specialist Kitty Bina, March 1999.

Secrets of Social Security numbers

"Cyberconspiracy Theories: Urban Legends are Snaring New Audiences on the Net Everyday," by L.A. Johnson, Pg. E-1, *Pittsburgh Post-Gazette*, July 30, 1998.

Big Lies on Campus

Psychic predicts massacre

"At USD, Massacre Rumor Means Harrowing Halloween," by Jeff Ristine, Pg. 1, Section B, *San Diego Union-Tribune*, October 31, 1998.

"Legend Haunting College Campuses," by Scott Powers, Pg. 5-C, *The Columbus (Ohio) Dispatch*, October 31, 1998.

Notes

Legends of the Silver Screen
The munchkin suicide
The Straight Dope, Cecil Adams, May, 1997.
"Really Most Sincerely, Still a Munchkin," by Leslie Doolittle, Pg. A2, *Orlando Sentinel*, October 29, 1996.
The Marisa Tomei Oscar mistake
"The Answer Man," by Roger Ebert, Pg. 5, Showcase Section, *Chicago Sun-Times*, June 15, 1997.
"And the Loser Is: Bad Oscar Rumor," The *Hollywood Reporter*, March 22, 1994.
"For Outstanding Achievement in the Art of Oscar Rumors," by David Sheehan, Pg. F2, *Orange County Register*, March 29, 1994.
The *Twister* tornado
"A Nobody in My Neck of the Woods," by Mark Steyn, Pg. 26, *London Daily Telegraph*, May 24, 1996.
A *Titanic* timeframe
"'Doctor Zzzhivago?' Many of This Season's Releases Have Epic Lengths, but That Doesn't Always Reflect Epic Visions," by Patrick Goldstein, Calendar Section, *The Los Angeles Times*, December 4, 1997.
Good Morning America transcripts, December 31, 1997 and January 15, 1998.
Disney secret messages
Movie Guide magazine, March, 1995.
"How a Rumor Spread About Subliminal Sex in Disney's 'Aladdin,'" by Lisa Bannon, Pg. A1, *The Wall Street Journal*, October 24, 1995.
Mouse Under Glass: Secrets of Disney Animation and Theme Parks, by David Koenig, Bonaventure Press, 1997.

Lawfully Wedded Legends
The philandering groom
Bold and the Beautiful, April 1999. Information reprinted with permission

Rumors in the Air Tonight
A killer "In the Air Tonight"
Parade magazine, "Walter Scott's Personality Parade," September 27, 1992.
311 and the KKK
"Schools Ban 311 Shirts," by Tony Moton, Pg. 37, *Omaha World-Herald*, April 19, 1996.
Information from *Knoxville News-Sentinel, USA Today, Spin, Rolling Stone*. Reprinted with permission.
Website statement quote. Reprinted with permission.
Beatles reunite on *Saturday Night Live*
Playboy Interview with John Lennon, January, 1981. Reprinted with permission.
"You Oughta Know" who this song's about
"Hell Hath No Fury Like Alanis Scorned," by John Sakamato, *Toronto Sun*, July 6, 1995.
Charles Manson and the Monkees
"Manson Madness" by Achy Obejas, Pg. 3, Section 5, *Chicago Tribune*, Feb. 19, 1999.

Cybermyths and Other Online Gossip
Nike shoe rebate
Quote from company statement. Reprinted with permission.
Blacks losing the right to vote
Statement from Dept. of Justice. Reprinted with permission.
"Online Hoax Prods Black Leaders Into Action," by Paul Shepard, *Associated Press*, December 2, 1998.
Bill Gates teams up with Disney
"On Spam: Wasting Time on the Internet," by Bill Gates, *The New York Times*, March 25, 1998.
"Bill Gates: An Urban Legend in his Own Time," by Don Crabb, Pg. 50, *Chicago Sun-Times*, February 15, 1998.

Notes

Shannon's Internet lesson
Interview with Bill Guillet, spokesman for Canton, N.C. Police Dept., March 1999.

Tall Tales of the Rich and Famous
Richard Gere and the gerbil
Palm Beach Post, September 5, 1995.
Mariah Carey's callous remark
"The Skinny on Mariah Hoax," by A.J. Benza,Pg. 24, New York Daily News, September 11, 1996.
Tiger Woods at the strip club
Milwaukee Journal, October 20, 1996.
"Foulline," by Steve Rosenbloom, Pg. 2, Sports Section, Chicago Tribune, October 28, 1996.
Tommy Hilfiger unfairly maligned
"Take a Spin Inside Tommy Hilfiger's Fashion Cuisinart," by Mimi Avins, Pg. 19, The Los Angeles Times Magazine section, August 25, 1996.
Statement from Tommy Hilfiger. Reprinted with permission.
Keanu Reeves marries David Geffen
"Keanu Sets the Record Straight," by Tim Allis, Pg. 65, 116-117, Out magazine, July/August, 1995.
Julia Child drops a duck
"Queen of Cuisine: Julia Child Continues to Reign Over the Hearts of Her Fans," by Alan Solomon, Pg. 7, Section 2, Chicago Tribune, May 10, 1995.
Marilyn Manson's Wonder Years
Transcript from E! Online website. Reprinted with permission.

Index

About the Author

For the last 12 years, Richard Roeper has written a daily column for the *Chicago Sun-Times*. The column is syndicated nationally by *The New York Times* Syndicate, and appears in such publications as the *Denver Post*, the *Arizona Republic* and the *Honolulu Star*. He has won the National Headliner Award as the outstanding newspaper columnist in the country, and has been honored by the Associated Press and the Illinois Press Association as the top columnist in Illinois.

Roeper has written for magazines such as *Entertainment Weekly*, *Spy*, *Playboy*, *TV Guide*, *New Woman* and *Chicago*, and he is the co-author of *He Rents, She Rents*, a guide to guy movies and chick flicks, which was published by St. Martin's Press in 1999.

Over the last 10 years, Roeper has hosted talk shows on radio stations WLS-AM, WLS-FM, WLUP-FM and WMVP-AM in Chicago. For the last six years, he has been a regular contributor on *Fox Thing in the Morning* on WFLD Fox-32 in Chicago. His commentaries have garnered one Chicago/Midwest Emmy and three nominations.

Roeper has appeared as a guest on *Nightline*, *Entertainment Tonight*, CNN, the E! Channel, NBC *Nightly News*, CBS *Evening News*, MSNBC, Fox News Channel and various PBS programs.

He is single and lives in Chicago.